GEMATRIA GEMS
Secret Code In The Bible Across Languages

Dedicated to my Grandparents,

Your resolve in the past has given me courage in the present.

Gematria Gems: Secret Code in the Bible Across Languages, by Zachary L. Goodwin, written and compiled by Zachary L. Goodwin 2018-2022.

© 2022 Zachary L. Goodwin

ILLUSTRATIONS:

Lord Gawad – Pgs. - 27, 32, 46, 47, 50, 63, 146, 232.

Zachary Goodwin – Pgs. - 23, 52, 55, 57, 93, 96, 133, 135, 137, 239.

All Rights reserved. No portion of this book may be reproduced in any form without permission from the publisher, except as permitted by U.S. copy right law. For permission contact:

GematriaGems@gmail.com

IBSN: 978-1-7371307-1-0

Paperback

TABLE OF CONTENTS

ALPHABETIC ORDER (**AO**)

A=1	B=2	C=3	D=4	E=5	F=6
G=7	H=8	I=9	J=10	K=11	L=12
M=13	N=13	O=15	P=16	Q=17	R=18
S=19	T=20	U=21	V=22	W=23	X=24
Y=25	Z=26				

NUMEROLOGY (**N**)

A=1	B=2	C=3	D=4	E=5	F=6
G=7	H=8	I=9	J=1	K=2	L=3
M=4	N=5	O=6	P=7	Q=8	R=9
S=1	T=2	U=3	V=4	W=5	X=6
Y=7	Z=8				

REVERSE ALPHABETIC ORDER (RAO)

Z=1	Y=2	X=3	W=4	V=5	U=6
T=7	S=8	R=9	Q=10	P=11	O=12
N=13	M=14	L=15	K=16	J=17	I=18
H=19	G=20	F-21	E=22	D=23	C=24
B=25	A=26				

REVERSE NUMEROLOGY (RN)

Z=1	Y=2	X=3	W=4	V=5	U=6
T=7	S=8	R=9	Q=1	P=2	O=3
N=4	M=5	L=6	K=7	J=8	I=9
H=1	G=2	F=3	E=4	D=5	C=6
B=7	A=8				

HEBREW GEMATRIA (HG)

6= ו	5= ה	4= ד	3= ג	2= ב	1= א
30= ל	20= כ	10= י	9= ט	8= ח	7= ז
90= צ	80= פ	70= ע	60= ס	50= נ	40= מ
600= ם	500= ך	400= ת	300= ש	200= ר	100= ק
			900= ץ	800= ף	700= ן

GREEK ISOPSEPHY (GI)

A=1	B=2	Γ=3	Δ=4	E=5	F=6
Z=7	H=8	Θ =9	I=10	K =20	Λ =30
M =40	N =50	Ξ =60	O =70	Π =80	P =100
Σ =200	T =300	Y =400	Φ=500	X=600	Ψ=700
Ψ =800					

WHAT IS GEMATRIA?

"What we call reality is in fact, nothing more than a culturally sanctioned and linguistically reinforced hallucination." – Terence Mckenna

This book is for people to learn the basic history, purpose, and spiritual roots of Gematria. Learn to examine world events, the dates, and people involved while keeping the concept of Gematria in mind. Every individual will be able to evaluate the context of any information being presented to them with Gematria if they wish. Gematria is a tool used through out time by many peoples and in no way should be considered a religion in itself. The oldest known example of Gematria is found back in the 8th century B.C.E, accredited to King Sargon II. *'The first use of gematria occurs in an inscription of Sargon II (727–707 B.C.E.) which states that the king built the wall of Khorsabad 16,283 cubits long to <u>correspond with the numerical value of his name.</u>'* ~ *Jewishvirtuallibrary.org.*

My goal is to pose questions for the reader to ponder while providing the reader with examples of Gematria. How is this tool from ancient times being used today? Why are numerical synchronizations so present? Why are numbers used in purposeful repetition? Are there codes in the bible? How would a code get its significance or origin?

There are so many concepts in life that we unfortunately, sometimes for reasons beyond our control, are unaware of. The desire to see the world as a place in harmony is an expression of the human desire to see order. The assumption that nature is rational is the basis of modern science and the reasoning underlying everyday life.

If you are informed about the use of Gematria, have knowledge of how to use the 4 base ciphers or if you desire to jump around to see the most personally eye-catching riddles feel free to. Be assured you can verify all information in the book for yourself. These links will make calculations much quicker if you have internet access.

Gematria Calculator – search: "Gematinator" http://gematrinator.com/calculator/index.php.

Date Calculations – search "Date to date calculator" https://www.timeanddate.com/date/duration.html

Do Words Have Power? - 3 And <u>God said</u>, "Let there be light," and there was light. 4 And God saw that the light was good. And God separated the light from the darkness. 5 God called the light Day, and the darkness he called Night. And there was evening and there was morning, the first day.
6 And <u>God said</u>, "Let there be an expanse in the midst of the waters, and let it separate the waters from the waters."

   As you have just read and maybe long believed, God **spoke** the world into existence. In the "Sepher Yetzirah" which translates from Hebrew to English as "The Book of Formation", this statement is on page 1, "God created His Universe by the three forms of expression: Numbers, Letters, and Words.".
   If the visible material universe is to be created by words, even as just humming vibrations, one needs letters to do so. This results in a language, that is readily and easily expressed letters, tones, vibrations, hums, or energies. Without biblical reference, think of what we were told as children, 'sticks and stones may break my bones but words will never hurt me'. But how true is this if we make childish songs to cope? Words do affect us and the tone, or vibration of the person speaking affects our susceptibility and reaction to what is being said. This is fact no matter how many times we sing this song as children or adults.

Today English is the most readily used language internationally thus it is unsurprising that English is registered as the most known language among the worlds population. In fact more people in China speak English than peoples in America. Those two countries alone register a considerable amount of earth's population. It's currently estimated that 360-400 million people speak English as a primary language, a larger 750 million speak English as a second language. The English language with **26** "letters" in the alphabet used to "spell" out any word in the world of the almighty, "God".

יהוה   **26** HG (YHVH)
"God" **26** Alphabetical Order
"Letter" **26** Numerology
"Spell" **26** Reverse Numerology
"Sound" **26** Reverse Numerology
"Heaven" **26** Reverse Numerology
"Atum" **26** Reverse Numerology
Atum is the Egyptian God of pre- existence and post-existence.

So now, are these simple yet profound synchronizations proof of God's interaction with us, proof of a simulation, or simply knowledge being given in riddles to those unaware?

Repetition is a tool used by all to help remember important details or new information. It's also a great tool for teaching. Think of all your favorite nursery rhymes and how often they repeat the same few phrases, words, or musical notes. In music theory certain chords elicit certain emotional responses in the listener. Think of every time you hear your favorite TV show's theme song playing and how if you were to hear that song out and about you would associate it with that show. Now everyone still compiles their own musical playlists and mix tapes so to the individual their choice of music still is up to them. Nevertheless popular shows have taken songs from relatively unknown bands and made them instantly recognizable because of the conscious repetition and association with the show. Now the song takes on a new meaning in the minds of the masses.

I would propose numbers affect us in a similar way in that, we are using numbers every day for our own purposes. Such as price tags, phone numbers, birthdays, addresses. Then on the other hand through media mediums, numbers and the words associated with them, are being impressed on the public. Such as 911, 101, 666. Popular religions have taken numbers of seeming obscurity and made them instantly recognizable because of the conscious repetition and association with the religious themes.

How It Works- The 4 ciphers will always be presented in the following order: Alphabetic Order (AO) also known as "Simple English Gematria", Numerology (N) also known as Pythagorean Gematria, Reverse Alphabetic Order (RAO), and Reverse Numerology (RN). The 4 base ciphers will always work in this way:

In the English language there are 26 letters. So naturally with the Alphabetic Order (AO.), A=1, B=2, C=3... Y=25, Z=26. Now for Reverse Alphabetic Order (RAO.) you will reverse the alphabet Z=1, Y=2, X=3... B=25, A=26. The Numerology (N.) cipher is inspired by Pythagoras. The idea is that a single digit represents a pure number, being there is only a single digit to interpret. A=1 B=2 C=3... Y=7(2+5=7), Z=8(2+6=8). For the Reverse Numerology (RN) cipher you explore the same idea of the numerology cipher but reverse the alphabetic order Z=1, Y=2, X=3... B=7(2+5=7), A=8(2+6=8).

For those eager to see proof take this simple but astounding example using the Alphabet Order (AO) G=7 O=15 D=4, 7+15+4=**26**. So "God" the name we use to describe the All is equal to the total amount of all the letters we have to communicate all our thoughts. With these 26 letters we can "spell" anything. If you use Reverse Numerology (RN.) S=8 P=2 E=4 L=6 L=6, 8+2+4+6+6=**26**.

Statistics & Probability- If you were to roll an evenly faced 26 sided dice numbered 1-26, 5 times and keep track of the sum of those 5 rolls, what would the odds be of you then rolling the same dice 5 times again and getting the same sum?

Using quick math, the max you could get is 130 and the minimum 5. So with 5 rolls you have $1/125$ chance of getting any given total, 0.8%. But what would be the odds of getting the same total after five rolls twice? $1/125 \times 1/125 = 1/15625 = 0.000064$. $0.000064 \times 100 = 0.0064\%$ are roughly the odds of any two five letter words equaling each other in the same cipher. There are actually only 12,478 five letter words in the English language which does reduce the amount of outcomes.

However, when the words being summed are relevant terms to each other it adds another layer of improbability that is incalculable. Also realize if after 5 rolls the dice resulted in the sum of 5 it would translate into "aaaaa". Again this changes the odds by an incalculable rate because of the rules and principles of the English language itself. In other words the dice example can only give us an idea of the probability of two words being equal to each other because the formula itself can not take into account the complexities of the English language. This deliberately points to the conclusion that certain dates, titles, and, names were chosen in English with Gematria in mind.

One must concede that using multiple ciphers does create a higher chance for getting a given total. However lets quickly observe how slim the odds are for two different five letter words being equal to each other throughout 4 different ciphers. Dice Example- $1/125 \times 1/125 = 1/15625$, but because we will be using four ciphers we now have to multiply those odds by 4 because the value was in one out of the four ciphers thus:
$4/125 \times 4/125 = 16/15625 = 0.001024$. Now take the total and multiply by 100 to find the percentage. $0.001024 \times 100 = 0.1024\%$ chance of occurring.

Observe, the correlating Gematria values of these correlating words that are 5 letters each. The first example of "Jesus" and "Cross" are given in the same cipher AO. The second example shows how "Judge" and "Gavel" have an overlap that occurs within the 4 ciphers we will stay in during this book

"Jesus" $10+5+19+21+19=$**74**. Alphabetic Order.
"Cross" $3+18+15+19+19=$**74**. Alphabetic Order.

"Judge" 47 AO. 20 N. 88 RAO. 25 RN.
"Gavel" 47 AO. 20 N. 88 RAO. 25 RN.

On December 27th, 2016 I observed a mathematical argument against Gematria put forth through computer calculations. Stating that for every number value there is an average of 587 words with that value. Ex: Jesus=74, and 74 likely has 586 other words to match it. Attempting to infer that this was proof of mere coincidence and over examination in the field of Gematria. However if one value has 587 pairs that is a very small amount comparatively. There are roughly 170,000 words in the English language. ~ *How many words do you need to speak a language. BBC.com.* Thus to find the probability of a word equaling another short hand one could divide 170,000 by the amount of 587 pairs according to the study.

587 / 170,000 = 0.00345294118

0.00345294118×100= 0.345924118% in one cipher.

"Jesus" **74** AO. <u>61</u> RAO. *34* RN.

"Cross" **74**. AO. <u>61</u> RAO. *34* RN

The Alphabetic Order cipher (AO) is also referred to as "Simple English Gematria" but the former is used in this book for easier memorization and reference. But notice how the standard name of the cipher itself is encoded.

"Simple" 19+9+13+16+12+5=**74** AO.

"English" 5+14+7+12+9+19+8=**74** AO.

"Gematria" 7+5+13+1+20+18+9+1=**74** AO.

Who is attributed as the first man with documented use of Gematria in history?

"Sargon" 19+1+18+7+15+14=**74** AO.

Opponents of Gematria's rational basis claim that;
1.With enough formulas in play you can make anything equal anything. This displays a lack of the concepts of probability. Not to mention most make such a claim before testing Gematria in their own studies. **2.**The study dabbles with interpreting divine aspects of numbers and in doing so commits blasphemy. Yet the holy books are numbered, versed, and characterized according to this practice. It would be hard to argue there aren't any cases of numbers used symbolically throughout the bible. Antagonist use these occurrences to 'disprove' the literalist interpretations. Published biblical scholars display the use of Gematria to the public and argue among themselves which Roman emperor was 'The Beast of Revelation' (pg. 80). Eliezar Ben Yose HaGelili a 2nd century rabbi, gave 32 rules to interpret the Tanakh, rule 29 is the use of Gematria.~ *Baraita of the Thirty-Two Rules.* Marcus the Valentinian a 2nd century church father, is reported to have used gematria when giving biblical interpretations.~ *The Theology of Arithmetic: Number Symbolism in Platonism and Early Christianity. Chs.harvard.edu.*
  3.Gematria is some form of magic or could be used in conjunction with occult rituals or divination. In their haste to sweep it under the rug the critic actually confirms that Gematria has power in its understanding (pg. 73). Unaware of the cognitive lapse they've suffered, the literalist deems to send the

truth seeker to hell for their seeking. If all knowledge or fruit in the garden, so to speak, is rooted in The One then all things in degree of good, evil, magical, or, mundane are rooted in God as well. Ask yourself if modern man has the capacity to learn the trade of 'coding', combining letters and numbers to create virtual realities, websites, games, and apps; what then is the Master of the Universe capable of with letters and numbers?

After a proper foundation of pattern association is developed new patters and new directions of thought previously inconceivable become ponderous. Once this is set forth in the study of Gematria, one can confront the intentions of those who choose to use the knowledge against those unaware. If the religious context from which this knowledge descends to us, truly points toward this aspect belonging to 'God', the Master Mathematician, then this knowledge indeed has power.

"What we call reality is in fact, nothing more than a culturally sanctioned and linguistically reinforced hallucination." 590 RN.
"Terence McKenna" 59 N.

RELIGION & SPIRITUALITY

This is **the key** chapter to pay attention to as most rituals and events that take place in our modern day and all throughout history get their foundation from biblical symbolism and myths of old. Thus I will be tying in modern day examples to show how things from the bible are played out by the same numerical contexts. If you want to follow along have your bible handy for verse references and an internet connection to personally verify all modern day and historical examples for yourself.

Gematria could be seen as drawing numerical parables between concepts, reality, and words. If you dive into sacred scriptures, myths, movies, or tabloid news for yourself with the **understood** tool of Gematria, you will see.

Mathew 13:10-13 ESV

"10 Then the disciples came and said to him, "Why do you speak to them in parables?" 11 And he answered them, "To you it has been given to know the secrets of the kingdom of heaven, but to them it has not been given. 12 For to the one who has, more will be given, and he will have an abundance, but from the one who has not, even what he has will be taken away. 13 This is why I speak to them in parables, because seeing they do not see, and hearing they do not hear, nor do they understand."

Christianity- Lets start by observing the titles and concepts centered around the Jesus figure. He gathered 12 disciples to travel with him to preach his "gospel". He was charged with "treason" against Rome by Rome's puppet ruler of Jerusalem at the time, Pontius Pilate. Jesus has the claim made for him, that he is the "messiah" which insinuated that he was King of Jerusalem, being in direct opposition to Roman rule. He was sentenced to death by crucifixion on a "cross". After his resurrection he cemented himself as part of the "Trinity". Christians insist that Jesus fulfilled the "Jewish" prophecies for the messiah figure. Theologically, Christ sits on a pole in direct opposition to "Lucifer", who carries similar Gematria. Hinting to a Hermetic belief apparently manifesting in our language and expressed in the axiom, 'As above so below, As below so above.' A fact that also holds true in the Gematria values of "God" and "Satan". Not to mention the words attributed to Jesus in 'The Lord's Prayer'.

Mathew 6:9-10 KJV

"9 After this manner therefore pray ye: Our father which art in heaven Hallowed be thy name. 10 Thy kingdom come, thy will be done in earth, as it is in heaven."

Thy will be done below (in earth) as it is above (in heaven).

"The Key Understood" **74** N.
"Jesus" **74** AO. <u>34</u> RN.
"Lucifer" **74** AO. <u>43</u> RN.
"Cross" **74** AO.
"Jewish" **74** AO.
"Mathematic Riddles" **74** N.
"Parables" **74** AO.
"Gospel" **74** AO.
"Messiah" **74** AO. <u>43</u> RN.
"Trinity" <u>43</u> N. **74** RAO.
"Forty Two" <u>43</u> N. **74** RAO. (pg. 37).

"Treason" <u>43</u> RN.
"Blasphemy" <u>43</u> RN.
"Death Of Jesus" <u>43</u> N.
4 pointed cross with 3 nails.
4×3=12, the 12 disciples.

The common numbers in these terms all have significant meaning. **74** the most reoccurring and a tribute linking him to God. Being that at the time and throughout most of history there was believed to be **7** planets and the agreed upon **4** elements of the world: 1.Moon, 2.Mercury, 3.Venus, 4.Sun, 5.Mars, 6.Jupiter, and **7**.Saturn; 1.Water, 2.Earth, 3.Air, and **4**.Fire, with God being the master of all. Thus it's fitting for the name of a 'god incarnate' figure to have a value of **74**. Also the name "Jesus Christ" is 11 letters long, as 7+4=11.

Seemingly juxtaposed numerically and spiritually to Jesus, the word "Beast" sums to **47** as well as "Sine". Like the sun sustains all life as it travels the sine wave around the earth. The sun's apparent path never escapes a measurable area around the earth. This area is between the two tropics of Capricorn and Cancer. When measuring from one tropic to the other, it measures to the tune of **47°**. Capricorn is approximately 23.5° South of the equator and Cancer is approximately 23.5° North of the equator.~ *How far apart in degrees are the Tropic of Cancer and the Tropic of Capricorn? Heimduo.org.* If the sine wave is duplicated, inverted, and overlapped, as to simulate viewing the suns course from both the southern and northern hemispheres, you get the symbol of balanced polarities or that which modern man ascribes to eternity. ∞.

"Beast" **47** AO.
"Sine" **47** AO.
"Time" **47** AO.
"Sins" **47** RAO.
"Vibration" **47** N.
23.5° from the equator to either tropic. 23.5×2 = **47**
Genesis **4:7** ESV
"If you do well, will you not be accepted? And if you do not do well, **sin is crouching at the door**. Its desire is contrary to you, but you must rule over it."

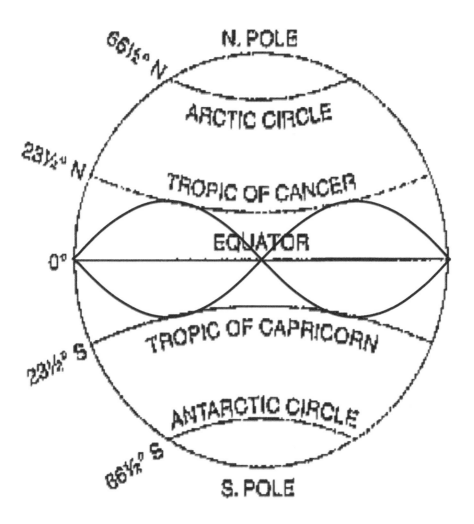

Christians believe the prophecies of the Old Testament were fulfilled by Jesus, his story told throughout the 4 gospels. So then it follows, Jesus is symbolically the link between the 3 'Trinity' and the 4 'Tetragrammaton', (יהוה). Notice how both concepts begin with a prefix in their wording, Trinity, Tetra-grammaton.

The 43/ 34 that appears in the list of words on pg.21 is not arbitrary to Jesus' life events. The cross being associated with the cycle of the four seasons, and God's son having his story told throughout 4 gospels. The cross can also be a symbol of the Trinity, with the stem symbolizing God touching down to earth and the three arms each symbolizing a deity of the trinity Father, Son, Holy Spirit.

Mathew 5:17 ESV
"Do not think that I have come to abolish the Law or the Prophets; I have not come to abolish them but to fulfill them."

Exodus 12:40 ESV
The time that the people of Israel lived in Egypt was 430 years.

Galatians 3:17 ESV
"This is what I mean: the law, which came 430 years afterward, does not annul a covenant previously ratified by God, so as to make the promise void."

"Treason" 43 RN.
"Blasphemy" 43 RN.
"Death Of Jesus" 43 N.
"Jesus Christ" 43 N.
"The Son Of God" 43 RN.
"Νόμος"   430 GI (Law)
April 3rd is a date written 4-3.

Add the three verses above, 517+1,240+317= *2,074*.

"Iesus Hominum Salvator" *274* AO
(Jesus Savior of Men)
On 25 December AD *274*, the Roman emperor
Aurelian established Sol Invictus as an official
religion.~ *Sol Invictus and Christmas.*
penelope.uchicago.edu.

   With the dates given in the bible a scientific study
published by The International Geology Review in
2012, concluded that the only two earthquakes they
could associate within the estimated time period of
Jesus crucifixion left them with the estimated date of
April 3rd, 33 A.D. that Jesus was killed.~ *Quake
reveals day of Jesus' crucifixion, researchers believe.
Nbcnews.com.* April 3rd when abbreviated is written
4-3 or 3-4. April 3rd is the **93rd** day of the year on the
Gregorian calendar.
Mathew 27:51 ESV
"And behold, the curtain of the temple was torn in
two, from top to bottom. And the earth shook, and
the rocks were split."

"Third of April" *73* N.
"Jesus King of the Jews" *73* N.
"Ritual Sacrifice" *73* N.
"Sacrifice" *73* AO.
73 total books in the Catholic bible
.

The Protestant bible, about the man from "Nazareth" who died on a "crucifix" to earn the title of "God's Son", begins at the **930**th chapter of the bible. Another fact is that God's sun, <u>averages</u> about **93,000,000** miles away from earth year round. This fact will become even more impressive when you research how all Christian holidays are in accordance with the solar calendar. For a brief taste, June 24th is dedicated to Saint John. Around June 24th, after the June solstice, the sun follows a lower and lower path through the sky, decreasing the span of the days as it passes through the summer into fall. It is until December 25th the sun then begins to rise after the winter solstice and the days begin to increase in time, symbolizing winter passing into spring.
John <u>3:3</u>0 KJV
"He must increase, but I must decrease."

"Crucifix" **93** AO.
"God's Son" **93** AO. <u>33</u> RN.
"Solar Man" **93** AO.
"Nazareth" **93** AO.
"The Word" **93** AO. <u>33</u> RN.
"Triclavianism" **93** RN.
"Thou art the Christ" **93** RN.
"The Law" **93** RAO.

The Easter holiday is symbolic of God's sun starting it's Right Ascension for the solar year. Notice that Right Ascension is often abbreviated as R.A. in astrology. Ra was the name of the Egyptian sun god of old. Coming out of the dark and fruitless death of winter the sun rises and begins new life or is reborn. The season of Spring takes its course as new natural life springs forth. 'The light at the end of the tunnel' reminds us that we can look back retrospectively, in the light.

John 8:12 "I am the light of the world."

The Egyptians had a similar holiday to Easter, Sham Al Nassim, celebrated in mid April- early May. Typically when they noticed the waters rise in the Nile. The month of April corresponds to the Hebrew month of Nissan. For muslims, the past few years have seen April take place during RAmadan. This physical RAising and rising of life is symbolized in the sun throughout all religions because it is true as far as man can tell. This notion of blooming after the dark winter or heaven after death has its root in the physical phenomena of man's ecosystem. This truth gives us hope that no matter how burning the troubles or dark the cold days we still move towards the season where we will inevitably bloom, bear fruit, and receive the harvest that we sowed.

Galatians 6:9 "And let us not grow weary of doing good, for in due season we will reap, if we do not give up."

Those who quest for Truth know that the words of Jesus elude to the very purpose of the quest.
John 8:32, "the truth shall set you free".
During this time of renewal of life it is normal to contemplate where life is headed, the only way to do this is to reflect on where we have been. As a result we have this Trinity of reflective thought. This is summed up in the Hebrew prayer " ויהיה הווה היה יהוה" which translates to English as 'God Past, Present, and Future.', this is later restated in, Revelation 1:8.
"I am the Alpha and the Omega," says the Lord God, "who is and who was and who is to come, the Almighty."

"I am the light of the world" **104** RN.
"The truth shall set you free" **104** N.
ויהיה הווה היה יהוה   **104** HG.
"Father, Son, Holy Spirit" **104** N.
"Who is and ever shall be" **104** RN.
"Zodiac" **104** RAO.

In the following verse we read Jesus spoke of 'the eye', as in singular. There has often been the association of a third eye or minds eye among the ancients. A symbol of enlightenment usually positioned in the center or crown of the head. Reminding of how the Kabbalistic Tree of Life displays this concept of light flowing to The Crown

(1), which is a single sphere on top of the figure, then down, where the next two spheres are side by side, like the eyes..(pg. 52). The idea that 'light' symbolizes a spiritual intelligence is further conveyed if you consider the halo of light depicted around many saintly figures of all traditions. This RAdiation of light conveyed that the eye was active and this spiritual discernment resulted in their saintly legend.

ESV Mathew 6:22-23 "<u>The eye is the lamp of the body</u>. If your eyes are healthy, your whole body will be full of light. 23 But if your eyes are unhealthy, your whole body will be full of darkness. If then the light within you is darkness, how great is that darkness!

"The eye is the lamp of the body" **271** AO. (271 is the **58**[th] prime)
"Pineal Gland" **58** RN.
"Biblical" <u>32</u> N. **58** RN
"The Eye" <u>32</u> N.
"Power" <u>32</u> N.

The ancients often reserved sun symbolism for the most high God(s). Overlaying a corresponding symbol on top of the sun is common among all religions. Now believing the body has 3 eyes and 5 senses, adding 3+5=8. 8 corresponding to the shape the sun makes throughout a year when observed at the same time each day, termed a *solar analemma.* Notice how the shape itself slightly resembles glasses or simply the eyes. ∞. Modern science understands the "iris" as a structure in the eye, responsible for controlling the diameter and size of the pupil, thus the amount of light reaching the retina. In our time the most common form a "viewer" receives any type of message, is through a "screen".

"Eye" **35** AO.
"Iris" **35** RN.
"Screen" **35** RN.
"Viewer" **35** RN.
"Watch Me" **35** RN.
"Ra" **35** RAO.
"Holy See" **35** N.
"Catholic" **35** N.
Genesis **3:5** ESV
'For God knows that when you eat of it your **eyes** will be opened, and you will be like God, knowing good and evil.'

"Eyes" <u>18</u> N. <u>18</u> RN.
"I" <u>18</u> RAO.
"Sun" <u>18</u> RN.
"IHS" <u>18</u> N. <u>18</u> RN.
Pg. 121.

Now Jesus was given the title Christ in Mark 8:29, this being declared by his disciple Peter, Jesus's response to this is rather telling. The reader will run into a problem when comparing Mark's account to the telling in Mathew. Jesus states "Flesh and blood has not revealed" that he was the messiah. It implies that only those 'in the know' or only the 'elect' could understand the Jesus mystery. To validate the Christian idea of the messiah being God or a demigod, or God in the flesh, or vice versa, some point to John 1:1.

Mark 8:29-30 KJV
"And he saith unto them, But whom say ye that I am? And Peter answereth and saith unto him, Thou art the Christ. 30 **And he charged them that they should tell no man of him**."
Mathew 16:16-17 ESV
"And Simon Peter answered and said, Thou art the Christ, the Son of the living God. 17 "And Jesus answered him, "Blessed are you, Simon Bar-Jonah! For flesh and blood has not revealed this to you, but my Father who is in heaven."
John 1:1 KJV
"In the beginning was the Word, and the Word was with God, and the Word was God.".

"The Word" **93** AO.
"Crucifix" **93** AO.

"Nazareth" **93** AO.
"God's Son" **93** AO.
"Triclavianism" **93** RN.
"Thou art the Christ" *213* AO. **93** RN.

Seeing that "thou art the Christ" equals 213 lets talk about a modern day ritual done around Christ symbolism. Tupac released an album <u>The Don Killuminati: The Seven Day Theory</u>, on the album cover is a black man on the cross. *"Tupac was the first rapper to depict himself on a cross, but he was not the last. Many rappers have depicted themselves as Jesus crowned with thorns, and many more have appropriated the themes of return, rebirth and resurrection." Tupac Shakur, Jesus and Resurrection Power. Huffpost.com.* The last album Tupac released was <u>"All Eyez On Me"</u> which released on February 13th, 1996 a date written **2-13**. Tupac was killed on September 13th, 1996. If you count the span of days from 2-13-96 to 9-13-96 it is exactly **213** days later. Tupac died from gunshot wounds after a "drive by shooting". His last album was released in February, known as "Black History Month". His mother was a political activist associated with the "Black Panther" party. Another relevant pairing of **213** and 74 is that, 74 days would convert into **2** months and **13** days.

"Drive By Shooting" **213** RAO.
"Black History Month" **213** AO.

"Black Panther" **213** RAO.

"Tupac Shakur" 139 AO. 139 is the 34th prime, like the 3-4 date for the death of Jesus.
"Jesus" 34 RN.
"Rapper" 34 RN.

Again the black man Tupac, first to portray himself as Christ, like the bible first gives the title 'Christ' to Jesus, stating "Thou art the Christ", 213 AO, dies from a "drive by shooting", 213 RAO, 213 days after his last album released on February 13th. Perhaps you chose to believe that Tupac had faked his death? Well you might get a chuckle from the fact Tupac released an album titled 'Machiavelli', and if you know anything about the real Machiavelli's history, then you know he faked his death to escape persecution. Tupac was murdered in Nevada, a state where it is legal to fake your own death.~ *Is It Legal to Fake Your Own Death. Courtroomproven.com.* Why is it that we see so many black men that are rappers associate themselves with Jesus symbolism? Let us turn to Gematria for insight into a reoccurring pattern with black men and Jesus.

"Jesus" **74** AO. 34 RN.
"Rapper" **74** AO. 34 RN.
"Nevada" 34 RN.

The first book of the "New Testament" is MATHew. Interestingly, the true authors of Mathew, Mark, Luke, and others are disputed with majority of the New Testament being written by Paul, who admittedly never met the man Jesus. Like 'Jesus', these are rather English sounding names which are uncommon in the areas of Jesus' gospel even today. We've covered how the name 'Jesus' with its link to **74** is significant. But how intellectually honest is it to pray to 'Jesus" if this wasn't his name? It may even be considered comedic to pronounce the name 'G-sus' when it is spelled with a J and the Hebrew name, ישוע would be pronounced, Yeshua. Going down this line of reasoning the question arises, "Why is the first book of the New Testament entitled 'Mathew'?"

"Mathematics" **112** AO. 40 N. 185 RAO. 68 RN.
"Catholicism" **112** AO. 49 N. 185 RAO. 68 RN.
1+1=2. Notice 112 with the Alphabetic Order.

What are the odds?
11 lettered words, 11x26= 286. 286-11, because 11 is the lowest possible total, 286-11= 275. 4/275x4/275= 16/75,625. However there are only 8,855, 11 letter words in english, 16/8,855= 0.18068876% chance of a pair, of 11 lettered words being equal in **one of** the four base ciphers.

In the first chapter of Mathew verses 1-17 there is the opening claim of the genealogy to Jesus, he states there are **42** generations from Abraham to Jesus. Tying in with the list below is a verse hinting to the appearance of Jesus in Revelation. Which is the 66th and final book of the bible. This is where the infamous 666 comes up, which we will decode later (pg.73). To continue the point with **42**, in Revelation 1:14-15 John describes seeing Jesus.

KJV Revelation 1:14 "His head and his hairs were white <u>like wool</u>, as white as snow; and his eyes were as a flame of fire;15 And <u>his feet like</u> unto fine <u>brass</u>, as if they burned in a furnace; and his voice as the sound of many waters." Hair of wool and feet of brass, some translations use the word "skin" in place of the word "feet".

"New Testament" **42** N. 66 RN. (The New Testament ends in the 66th book)
"Math" **42** AO.
"Savior" **42** N.
"Sin" **42** AO.
"Nazareth" **42** N.
"Emmanuel" **42** RN.
"Septuagint" **42** N.

Be aware there is an ancient list of negative confessions dated around 1250 BC. The list is known as 'The **42** Laws of Ma'at", the first confession of the

42 is "I have not committed **sin**". Not contrary the ancient name of what we call Egypt was pronounced 'Khem-Mat'. We now see how the number **42** ties into Jesus himself, whom many scholars will argue was of dark complexion, not the straight haired white man he is most often portrayed as. However I will concede that different parts of the world may have the same deity but represent that deity different, but the point is if one is to entrust their eternal soul into something or someone, shouldn't they have the most accurate description of such before doing so?

42 is often paired with 59 being that February, often referred to as Black History Month ends on the 59th day of the year. And since the modern day public schools like to 'teach' us about the American Civil War for 12 years straight you should remember what day the American Civil War ended. The Civil War ended on May 9th, 1865 a date that can be written 5-9. Had you noticed that the American Civil War began on April 12, 1861? April 12th is the *102nd* day of the year, *102* being another reoccurring number with Black Historical Events. The amount of connections one can discover from observing these three numbers will lead to innumerable discoveries on the topic.

I'd like to again remind of the importance of Prime Number relationships. **181** is the **42nd** prime number, from the first black president, Barack Obama's birthday, August 4th to the first day of black history month February 1ˢᵗ is **181** days. "Jackie" Robinson who wore the number **42** is largely considered the first African American in white major league. However be aware there was a black man who played before him by the name of "Moses Walker". Moses Walker is not recognized as the first because he didn't complete a full season and only played in **42** games.~ *Moses Fleetwood Walker. Lemelson.mit.edu.* Let us now shed light on some terms from the English language that are associated with black people in light of this information.

"February" **42** N.
"Black History" **181** RAO.
"Barack Hussein Obama II" **181** AO.
181 Is the **42ⁿᵈ** prime number
"Tuskegee" **42** RN.
"Jackie" **42** RN.
"Moses Walker" **42** N.
"Nigger" **42** N. *102* RAO.
"Slavery" *102* AO. **42** RN.

"Slave" *59* AO. *76* RAO.
"Negro" *59* AO. *76* RAO.
"Blues" *59* AO. *76* RAO.
"Rasta" *59* AO. *76* RAO.
The 'Million Man March' took place on October 16ᵗʰ the day that leaves *76* days left in the year.
"The White Lion" *59* RN.

While this information alone can be very eye opening we will take a more detailed look into modern political racism examples later. But for now lets examine a modern day Sports event with relevant prophecy from the New Testament in Acts *7:6*.

Acts *7:6* ESV
"And God spoke to this effect—that his offspring would be sojourners in a land belonging to others, who would enslave them and afflict them <u>four hundred years</u>."

In 1619 the first slaves arrived in modern day United States on a ship named "The White Lion", <u>400</u> years from then was the year 2019. Think of symbolism that has occurred in short time since with the Black Lives Matter movement gaining national recognition and the first woman of color elected as Vice President. Not to mention that ESPN declared on September 2nd, 2019 that it was "The year of the black quarter back".~ *The Undefeated Presents: The Year of the Black QB. Espn.com.* At the conclusion of the 2019-2020 season, the black QBs; Lamar Jackson, won the leagues MVP award and Patrick Mahomes won the NFL Super Bowl. After the conclusion of the Super Bowl Mahomes had a career total of <u>76</u> touchdowns. Later on July 6th, a date that can be written <u>7-6</u>, Mahomes signed the largest contract extension in the history of the N FL. The contract was reportedly "worth more than $400 million" per CNBC.~ *Patrick Mahomes' 10-year extension with Kansas City Chiefs is worth more than $400 million. Cnbc.com.*

   Another ritual conducted around the same numbers, involved arguably the most famous African American, **44**[th] U.S. President "Barack Obama". In light of the prophecy being in the book of Acts and this ritual involving the **44**[th] president, realize Acts is the **44**[th] book in the Bible. November 17th leaves **44** days left in the calendar year and on November 17th, 2020 Obama released the book "A Promised Land". This phrase is associated with the bible when "Abraham" is promised a land by God, and not arbitrary is the following verse of Acts 7:7.

"Barack Obama" _76_ RN.
"A Promised Land" _59_ N. _76_ RN
"Negro" _59_ AO. _76_ RAO.
"Slave" _59_ AO. _76_ RAO.
"Abraham" **44** AO. (Abraham, the one commissioned "A Promised Land" by God)

Acts 7:7 ESV
"But I will judge the nation that they serve,' said God, 'and after that they shall come out and worship me in this place."
"United States" 77 RN.

One of many parables between Jesus or YESHua and the sun is seen in the Hebrew roots of the words. Picture the colors white and black, Yesh and Ayin, something and nothing. Yesh means, simply, everything that there is, Ayin is Nothing.

Genesis 1:3-4 ESV

"3 And God said, "Let there be light," and there was light. 4 And God saw that the light was good. And God separated the light from the darkness."

Zohar – Translation by Nurho De Manhar.

"In the beginning" was Ayin Soph, the Divine, the self-existent infinite begin, without likeness or reflection, the incomprehensible, the unknowable One, the blessed and only Potentate, the King of Kings and Lord of Lords. who only hath immortality, dwelling in Light which no man can approach unto, whom no man hath seen or can see, before whom the great archangel with face beneath his wings bends in lowly reverence and adoration, crying, "Holy! Holy! Holy! who art and was and evermore shall be."

Consider how when one says the English word 'Yes', one often moves the head up and down, just as the sun travels up in to the day and down into the night, confirming reality. White and black are symbolic of opposing forces and also oppose each other on the color spectrum. These two hold every possibility of hue and coloring between them in the spectrum. The merging of the two could be symbolized as a flame diving into water. Our sun helping to generate life which many will argue sprang from the murky depths. We do know that all life became more diversified than ever after the enormous melting ice caps post Ice Ages. ~ *"Krause said. "During the Glacial Maximum, diversity got lost." But then came a period called the Bølling-Allerod "interstadial" (interstadials are relatively warmer periods during ice ages), beginning about 14,500 years ago. Ice sheets retreated, and indeed, this is when humans crossed the land bridge from Asia to North America…. But it seems likely that warmer conditions helped the event happen. At the same time, Krause noted, forests were regrowing across Europe… Climate shifts dramatically upended the lives of prehistoric humans, scientists say. Washingtonpost.com.* We know that man himself is composed of roughly 70% water. The moon has the power to pull waves of the ocean and all bodies of water to some degree. Water alone can shape rock when at great pressure as seen on display at the Grand Canyon. We tend to correlate the shades of blue with water. The sun however holds power to diversify all life to innumerable degrees. To maintain its perfect distance promotes life as we know it. An uncontrolled flame burns away everything as it spreads, yet the absence of a fire in the harsh wilderness of space would create a void of coldness and fear. Light is associated with the color yellow because of the suns glow. The last primary color Red appears as the only color all humans share regardless of Race, the color of blood.

   The same parable comes from the Egyptian stories in the forms of Atum and Apep. The Great Snake of Darkness that refused to let the Light leave his grip. This analogy is expanded upon with the rivalry of Horus and Set. One fighting to shine for all the Hours of the day (Horus), while the other looked to make darkness Set forever entering humanity into "chaos" (Set). From the Greek myths we encounter "Typhon" and Zeus.

Typhon – By Mike Greenberg, PhD
Typhon stole Zeus's greatest weapons and began his chaos on Olympus. Against the great monster and the power of Zeus's thunderbolts, the gods were forced to flee. Zeus tried to fight back against Typhus, but without his weapons was overcome. Typhus stole the sinews from Zeus's legs, rendering the king virtually helpless.

"Set" **19** RN.
"Typhon" **19** RN.
"Chaos" **19** N.
(pg. 174).

   In English we say 'sun', the Hebrew translation is rendered שֶׁמֶשׁ (She mesh). When the first letter שׁ

has a dot above on the right side it is the SH sound. We know the association of the right and its use to confirm or approve, corresponding to the Shhh sound. KJV Psalm 46:10 "Be still, and know that I am God: I will be exalted among the heathen, I will be exalted in the earth." When the letter שׁ has a dot to the top left it is pronounced (SS), the sound a snake makes. As if to denote that the left side is negative and predisposed to sin. Not to far back in history it was common for those who were left handed to be deemed witches or other types of incarnated evil. To the same note the Hebrew word סָמֶךְ (Semekh) means 'support', as the sun supports life. If we look at the first Hebrew letter in the word semek, ס, it looks similar to the sun and the course it travels on for eternity. One may also see an ouroboros, the snake eating its own tail. The ouroboros long being associated with the milky way and the concept of cycles throughout eternity, or the circle of life. The Divine Man and the Beast, the Light of the Sun and darkness of space, good and evil, order and chaos.

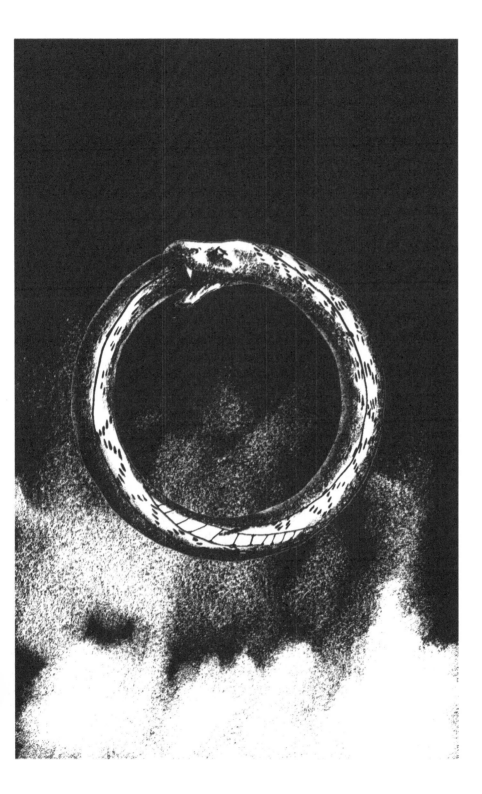

A book of Greek myths about their sun god Helios would be referenced to as, "Helios Biblios" meaning in English "Sun Book". But is Hell a burning place, with all this positive sun symbolism involved in all religions? Notice the public derives from Helios Biblios, Holy Bible. The writers of ancient scriptures were well versed in allegory and correspondence between the natural world and man. All who approach the scriptures in this view can gain from any sect of religious scripture they delve, as encouraged in the bible.

2nd Corinthians 3:6 "not of the letter but of the Spirit. For the letter kills, but the Spirit gives life."

"The Word" **39** N.
"The Letter Kills But The Spirit Gives Life"
167 N. (167 is the **39th** Prime Number)

In a similar fashion the letters of the Tarot card below, when read right to left like Hebrew, renders the word 'Tora'. The 'Torah' is the laws of God as revealed by Moses. However, when reading left to right the wheel displays the word 'Taro', reminding of the Egyptians, and how the constellation 'Taurus', a sacred bull that was associated with the cycle of life in spring. Giving insight into the characters and archetypes involved, being that. If you chose to start at the R instead the word 'Rota' can be rendered. All this attributed to the 'wheel' of fortune.

~ It is not even known the origin of the term tarot, different explanations have attributed the following languages. Egyptian (from tar, path, and ro, region); Indo Tartar (tan, tara, zodiac); Hebrew (torah, law); Latin (resulting from the combination of the word rota, and orat; speaking wheel); even Taoist and Chinese. Tarotinstitute.com.

"Tarot" **74** AO.
"Occult" **74** AO.
"Wheel of Fortune" **74** N.

החוקים	169 HG. (The Laws)
סִפְרֵי תוֹרָה	961 HG. (Books of Torah)

"Ancient Mystery Religions" 322 RAO.
"Mathematical Proof of God" 223 AO.

"Jesus" 74 AO.
"Beast" 47 AO.

The Words of Christ– Let us dive into some of the
most powerful quotes that are attributed to Jesus. I
only say 'attributed' as a disclaimer due to the fact
that the scholarly consensus is that the stories and
quotes first recorded in the gospel of Mark, are an
estimated 30-50 years after Jesus death. The main
reason to that being that most disciples believed the
time of the 2nd coming would be soon thus there was
no need to write all the exploits down. Things to
keep in mind when researching the 'powerful'
teachings of God's sun.

"Power" *77* AO. **32** N. 58 RAO. <u>22</u>. RN
"Christ" *77* AO. **32** N.
"Shemesh" *77* AO. **32** N. (Hebrew name for the sun)
"Meditate" *77* AO. **32** N.
There are 7 vowels in english, 7 musical notes in a
scale, and 7 colors in a naturally occurring rainbow.

"Biblical" **32** N. 58 RN.
"Zodiac" 58 AO. **32** RN.
"America" **32** N. (America was established 7-4-
1776. (7+4+1+7+7+6= **32**).
"Helios" **32** N. (Greek name for the sun)
"<u>Life</u>" **32** AO. <u>22</u> RN. There are **32** paths of wisdom
on the Kabbalistic Tree of <u>Life</u>.

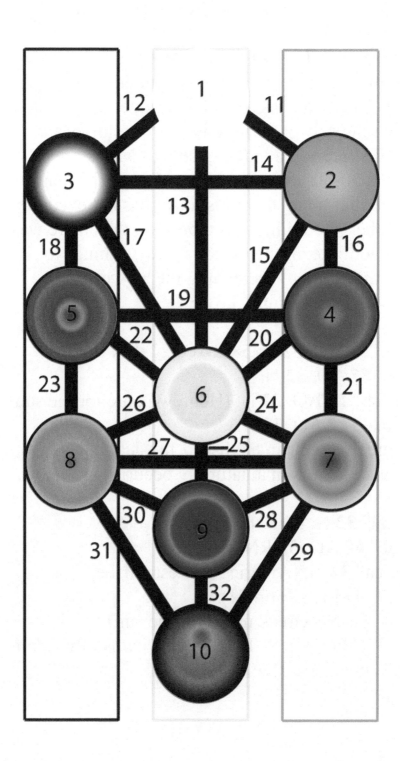

The 22 in "power" is also interesting in light of the New Testament being glued to the back of the Tanakh or Old Testament, be aware there are 22 letters in the Hebrew alphabet. According to the testimony in Exodus 3:14, God spoke in Hebrew declaring "I WILL BE WHAT I WILL BE". In the English bible it often translates as "I AM". Never forget the core concept of the study is that God created the world with Numbers, Letters, and Words.

"I Am" 58 RAO. 22 RN.
"Power" 58 RAO. 22. RN

Kabbalah can be translated as "to receive", the philosophy is concerned with inner wisdom. How is one to receive wisdom that they don't already have from within? This is what the Kabbalah student is concerned with, the art of receiving. The most common symbol used is the Tree of Life, which is a visual representation of a path of return to God. The Tree can be used as a template or framework to find correspondences in multiple systems. Kabbalah is a long enduring philosophy, much longer than the popular book "The 48 Laws of Power". Something esoterically interesting is the structure of the English words, 'receive' and 'believe'. Note how the middle part of both words is verbalized as (e v e), but the I and the E switch places. Thus when one does beLIEve, they convince themselves of something they are not entirely sure of. However one can verify, that which has been received.

There was a total of **48** male prophets who received the words that composed the Tanakh.
"To Receive" **48** N.
"Manifest" **48** RN.
גדולה   **48** HG (Greatness, Majesty, Renown)
חיל   **48** HG (Force, Power, Might)
223 is the **48**th Prime Number in sequence of Primes. (pg. 60).

Going back to **77**, lets focus on an instrument of "power", a sword. The **7**th letter of the Hebrew alphabet is Zayin. Zayin is referred to as the "sword bearer" of God. The letter does resemble somewhat of a sword or spear. In fact the letter is used by itself to represent a 'weapon' or a 'tongue'. Catholics are familiar with Mary being depicted as pierced by **7** swords.~ *Litany of Our Lady of Seven Sorrows. Catholic.org*. We see in Mathew 10: <u>34</u>-<u>36</u> Jesus claims he came to bring the sword, many bibles will subtitle this passage "Not Peace but a Sword". While this is contrary to the Jewish prophecies concerning the messiah, Isaiah 2:4, many people enjoy the idea of Jesus being a revolutionary or counter culture figure of the times. The sword can also be seen as a symbol that expresses the concept of 'no pain, no gain'. As זין means 'sword', the same root word appears in מזון meaning 'food'. There are no spoils of war without bloodshed, there is no repair from surgery without the doctor cutting the patient open, there is no resurrection without the crucifixion. These concepts in mind, remember the '7 cries on the cross' and read the 7 words Jesus uses to describe his atoning achievement, Mathew 27:46 "My[1] God[2], My[1] God[2], why[3] have[4] you[5] forsaken[6] me[7]".

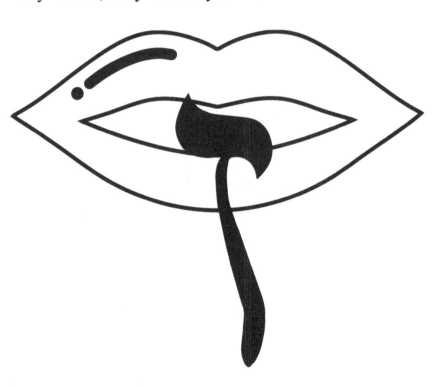

"Not Peace But A Sword" 67 N.
זין   67 HG (Zayin)
"Watch Your Mouth" 67 N.

Zayin is the 7th letter

Mathew 10 Verses 34-36.   34+36=**70**

"Sword Bearer" **70** RN.

"And a persons enemies will be those of his own household" **700** RAO.

"Sword" 79 AO. (7+9=16 = 1+6= **7**)

"Sword" 25 N. (2+5= **7**)

"Power" *77* AO. 58 RAO. 22 RN.

"Mouth" *77* AO. 58 RAO. 22 RN.

Mathew 10:34-36 ESV

34"Do not think that I have come to bring peace to the earth. I have not come to bring peace, but a sword.35 For I have come to set a man against his father, and a daughter against her mother, and a daughter-in-law against her mother-in-law. 36 <u>And a person's enemies will be those of his own household.</u>

Revelation 2:16 ESV

Therefore repent. If not, I will come to you soon and war against them with <u>the sword of my mouth</u>.

Revelation 19:15 ESV

"<u>From his mouth comes a sharp sword</u> with which to strike down the nations, and he will rule them with a rod of iron. He will tread the winepress of the fury of the wrath of God the Almighty."

Proverbs 18:21 ESV

Death and life are in the power of the tongue.

April 12th, 1922
"My feelings as a Christian points me to my Lord
and Savior as a fighter. It points me to the man who
once in loneliness, surrounded by a few followers,
*recognized **them** for what they were and summoned*
*men to fight against **them** and who, God's truth was*
greatest not as a sufferer but as a fighter. In
boundless love as a Christian and as a man I read
through the passage which tells us how the Lord at
last rose in His might and seized the scourge to drive
out of the Temple the brood of vipers and adders.
Today, after two thousand years, with deepest
emotion I recognize more profoundly than ever
before the fact that it was for this that He had to
shed his blood upon the Cross."
-Adolf Hitler~ Munich, Speech of April 12th, 1922.
Hitler.org.

Certainly, one of the most famous claims made in all the bible comes to us in Mathew **7:7**.

Mathew **7:7** ESV

"Ask, and it will be given to you; seek, and you will find; knock, and it will be opened to you."

Many doubters will say something along the lines of 'I asked for x and didn't get it therefore this religion is false', for which christians have developed many apologetics. However, in this short statement many "secrets are revealed". As many seekers of knowledge will attest, those who seek often do find, inspiring the origin of the rejoiceful phrase 'Eureka'. When you read Mathew 7:7 in the English Standard Version of the bible and include Mathew 7:8 you find a marvelous synchronicity. Using this same method when you decode the infamous verse of Genesis *3:22* will give similar insights. Strikingly

the word "Genesis" sums to 78, and Genesis *3:22* is
the 78th verse of the bible

"Secrets Are Revealed" *77* N..
"Learn Good and Evil" *77* N.
"Power" *77* AO.
"Christ" *77* AO.
"Mouth" *77* AO.

"Ask, and it will be given to you; seek, and you will
find; knock, and it will be opened to you. 8 For
everyone who asks receives, and the one who seeks
finds, and to the one who knocks it will be opened."
707 N.

"Knowledge is Power" 78 RN
"Genesis" 78 AO.

   As it is stated you must 'ask' in order to receive.
This inevitably results in the debate of if prayers
should be made aloud or silently. With the word
"mouth" having the sum of 77 it would be
reasonable to conclude that Mathew 7:7 is
encouraging the vocalizing of prayers. Or could it be
the hidden message of ask and you will receive is
that we have already received our power, the
knowledge of good and evil? What good are our acts
if we don't know our own intentions?

The dual 7s corresponding to "power" could also be tied into the opening story of creation and expulsion in the garden. It takes God 7 days to create the world, and it was good. Then at the end of the 7 days Adam and Eve ate the fruit and thus "learn good and evil". Once this power is learned, according to God, in Genesis *3:22* KJV "And the LORD God said, Behold, the man is become as one of us, to know good and evil: and now, lest he put forth his hand, and take also of the tree of life, and eat, and live for ever."

"And the LORD God said, Behold, the man is become as one of us, to know good and evil" *322* RN.
"Abrahamic Religions" *322* RAO.
"The Children of Israel" *322* RAO.
"Ancient Mystery Religions" *322* RAO.

"Mathematical Proof of God" *223* AO.
"A Key To The Universe" *223* AO.
"The Key Understood" *223* N.
"The Miraculous Catch Of One Hundred And Fifty Three Fish" *223* N.

The next passage covered implies a miracle done in the presence of Jesus in the 21st chapter of John, indeed it is referred to as "the miraculous catch of one hundred and fifty three fish". One of many of miracles performed by Jesus in this book properly named "Holy Bible" or simply "The Bible". When I say properly named it's not sarcasm but in reality this is the name of the book passed down to us and it was named with Properties.

"Geometry" <u>45</u> N.
"Holy Bible" <u>45</u> N. **153** RAO. <u>45</u> RN.
"The Bible" **153** RAO. <u>45</u> RN
"The Illuminati" **153** AO.
"Jesuit Order" **153** RAO.

"The Miraculous Catch" *74* RN.
"Christ Jesus" *74* RN.
"Masonic" *74* AO.

John 21:1-11 ESV
After this Jesus revealed himself again to the disciples by the Sea of Tiberias, and he revealed himself in this way **2** Simon Peter, Thomas (called the Twin), Nathanael of Cana in Galilee, the sons of Zebedee, and two others of his disciples were together.**3** Simon Peter said to them, "I am going fishing." They said to him, "We will go with you." They went out and got into the boat, but that night they caught nothing.**4** Just as day was breaking, Jesus stood on the shore; yet the disciples did not know that it was Jesus. **5** Jesus said to them, "Children, do you have any fish?" They answered

him, "No." **6** He said to them, "Cast the net on the right side of the boat, and you will find some." So they cast it, and now they were not able to haul it in, because of the quantity of fish. **7** That disciple whom Jesus loved therefore said to Peter, "It is the Lord!" When Simon Peter heard that it was the Lord, he put on his outer garment, for he was stripped for work, and threw himself into the sea.**8** The other disciples came in the boat, dragging the net full of fish, for they were not far from the land, but about a hundred yards off. **9** When they got out on land, they saw a charcoal fire in place, with fish laid out on it, and bread. **10** Jesus said to them, "Bring some of the fish that you have just caught." **11** So Simon Peter went aboard and hauled the net ashore, full of large fish, **<u>153</u>** of them. And although there were so many, the net was not torn.

This ancient tale may be why many Greek Christians supported the Symbol of the fish inscribed with "ΙΧΘΥΣ" pronounced in English (ichthys). This is an acronym for "Ἰησοῦς Χριστός, Θεοῦ Υἱός, Σωτήρ" pronounced in English as (Iēsous Christos, Theou Yios, Sōtēr), which translates into English as 'Jesus Christ, Son of God, Savior'. In light of Jesus being seen as one with God, know the Hebrew word for fish is "דג" pronounced Da-g. In Hebrew you read from right to left, doing so to the English transliteration above would thus be 'G-ad', rather close to 'God'. This symbol can also be interpreted as the center of the **Vesica Piscis** a sacred geometry symbol which can be interpreted as the womb we are all brought forth from. In the case of Jesus, the womb of the virgin mother Mary. Another interpretation could be that the two outer circles are 'The Father' and 'The Holy Spirit' with the intersection being 'God's Son'. To the left is severity and to the right is mercy, Jesus instructs to cast the net to the right.

There is a mathematical formula to calculate the measuring of the oval shape formed by the intersection of the two disks. The mathematical ratio of the height to the width across its center is the square root of three or √3. √3= 1.73205081. It can also be calculated by 265÷**153**= **1.7**3202614. If you round to the nearest decimal you will get **1.7** for both formulas. ~*Vesica Piscis. Formulasearchengine.com.* Interesting as **153** is the **17**th 'Triangular Number', meaning whatever number in the sequence you want to know simply add from 1 up to the number, in this case **17**.
(1+ 2+3 +4+5+ 6+7+8+ 9+10+11+12+13+14 +15+16+17) = **153**. Because we added all prior numbers up to **17** and it summed to **153**, thus **153** is the 17th 'Triangular Number'.

"Miraculous Catch" *59* N.
"Freemasonry" *59* RN.
59 is the 17th Prime in sequence of Prime Numbers.

"God" 17 N.
"Mason" 17 N.
Modern freemasonry was established in 1717, which coincidentally was *59* years before the establishment of America in 1776.

7 disciples witnessed the miracle, 17 is the 7th Prime in sequence of Prime Numbers.

7 is the 4th Prime in sequence of Prime Numbers.
If you add up the first four Primes in the sequence of
Prime Numbers: 2+3+5+7= 17.

Mathew 4:19 ESV
"Follow me, and I will make you fishers of men."
413 AO.
The divisors of 413 are: 1, 7, 59, 413.

   This is all attributed to the sacred geometry symbol
the **Vesica Piscis** a manifestation of mathematics.
Another mathematical and physical correspondence
with the symbol occurs in American Football. Where
the center of the symbol is the shape of the ball.
There can only be 53 men on an NFL roster at one
time. The standard Football field is 53 yards wide.

"Vesica Piscis" *53* N.

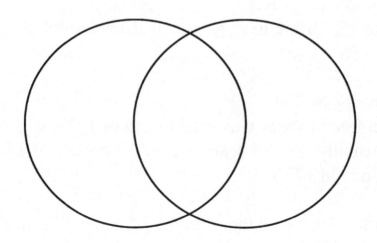

"Bring Forth" **153** RAO.
"Unconscious" **153** AO.
"Push And Pull" **153** RAO.
"Jesuit Order" **153** RAO

This Christian symbol shares resemblance with the fish in that in the center of the sun "IHS" is inscribed inside of its 32 rays. However this symbols true meaning is somewhat obscured by the multiple interpretations attributed to it. "IHS" being the first letters (iota-eta-sigma) of the name Jesus in the Greek alphabet: ΙΗΣ. From there and perhaps inspired by the Greek acronym the Romans created their own, *Iesus Hominum Salvator* - 'Jesus, Savior of Men'. Some argue that the symbol is not one used by the church itself but instead originating with the 'Jesuit Order'. Also known as the 'Society of Jesus' which is interesting in light of the same letters used for this acronym, *Iesus Humilis Societas* - 'Humble Society of Jesus'. Another inclination is that IHS – represents Isis, Horus, and Set all Egyptian figures. Isis representing the divine feminine, the Ayin from which Yesh materializes. Her two sons, being the two polarities battling each other for superiority Horus and Set. Here we see the two polarities of the outer circles and their manifestation coming from the intersection. Notice the 32 Rays emerging from the sun in the image. Funny enough its the churches and institutions feigning moral superiority that use the association of ancient symbols with their logos and their gods. One more thing to always remember with symbolism, 'As above so below'.

Exodus 20:4 KJV "Thou shalt not make unto thee any graven image, or any likeness *of any thing* that *is* in heaven above, or that *is* in the earth beneath, or that *is* in the water under the earth:"

"Horus" 27 N. 54 RAO. 27 RN.
"Sun" 54 AO. 27 RAO.

"Jesuit" **84** AO. 42 RN.
"Iesus Humilis Societas" **84** RN.

"Iesus Hominum Salvator" 122 RN.
"Pope Francis" 122 AO.
Pope Francis is the 1st publicly Jesuit Pope.

"Satan" *80* RAO.
"Sun God" *80* AO

An important quote attributed to Jesus that one should consider is presented in Mark 12:28-30. When asked if there was one thing that is most important to God and thus the religion of Christianity Jesus said;
Mark 12:30 KJV
"And thou shalt love the LORD thy God with all thy heart, and with all thy soul, and with all thy mind, and with all thy strength: this is the first commandment."

If you add the numbers of the verse 12:30 (12+30=**42**) realizing this quote attributed to the "savior" of "mankind's" "sin".

"Savior" **42** RN.
"Mankind" **42** RN.
"Sin" **42** AO.
"Nazareth" **42** RN.
"Emmanuel" **42** RN.

"Love the Lord your God with all your heart and with all your soul and with all your mind and with all your strength"
450 N.
"Holy Bible" *45* N. *45* RN.
"The Bible" *45* RN.

"And thou shalt love the LORD thy God with all thy heart" 206 N.
"God" 26 AO
יהוה 26 HG

After we read Jesus restating the first commandment as the most important and to, it may dawn on you how Jesus is often portrayed with the 'Sacred Heart' or pointing towards his heart in Christian artwork. While one hand points toward the heart the other points above. This pose focuses the observers eyes on the 7th Chakra, Crown and the 4th

Chakra, Heart. Example ~ *The Cristo De La Misericordia, or the Christ of Mercy Statue, 2009, Nicaragua.*

"Christ of Mercy Statue" *112* RN.
"Cristo De La Misericordia" *112* N.

.

Mathew **9:4** ESV
"But Jesus knowing their thoughts said "Why do you think evil in <u>your hearts</u>"
"Heart Chakra" **94** AO. **49** N.
"Your Heart" **49** RN.
"Emotional" **49** RN.
"Green" **49** AO.
The Heart Chakra is most often depicted as green.

"Do Things Out Of Love" *227* AO.
227 is the **49**th Prime in sequence of Prime Numbers.

Another quote not as often referenced by trinitarian Christians comes to us in the book of Mathew chapter **19** verse 17. When called good master or teacher, depending on translation, Jesus is asked what good things must one do to enter heaven? This implying that Jesus has the power or knowledge of how to accomplish the task and also deem others appropriate to enter. KJV Mathew **19**:17 "And he said unto him, Why callest thou me good? there is none good but one, that is, God: but if thou wilt enter into life, <u>keep the commandments.</u>"

"<u>Keep the commandments</u>" 309 RAO. *93* RN.
"Crucifix" *93* AO.
"God's Son" *93* AO.
"The Word" *93* AO. 39 N.

"None good but one" **67** N.
"Good" **67** RAO.
67 the 19th Prime in sequence of Prime Numbers, the words are used in Mathew chapter 19. (pg. 108).

I hope this brief examination into some of the quotes and stories in the gospels was fruitful for you but we will now continue on to the concluding book of the bible Revelation. In the following verse is condensed a wealth of historical and occult knowledge. Before we begin to taste the fruits of this knowledge let us first set the table. The English word 'wisdom' is rendered as חכמה (**Chokhmah**) in Hebrew. In the Masoretic Texts, which is the authoritative Hebrew Aramaic text of the 24 books of the Tanakh in Rabbinic Judaism, the word "Chokhmah" appears *149* times.~ *What is Chokhmah. Slife.org.*

"Chokhmah" *149* RAO.
"Revelation" *149* RAO.

The symbolic amount of times the word appears in correlation with its Gematria value implies that some wisdom indeed lies within the interpretation and understanding of Gematria values. Thus "let the one who has <u>understanding</u> *calculate* the number". The word calculate merely being inserted to insure one knows what is required. Continuing with backdrop knowledge, the Greeks indeed used and understood the significance of Gematria, however they used the term "Isopsephy" to name the practice (pg. 124). And this verse in the "New Testament" is a Greek Isopsephy riddle. Now remember "Revelation" is the <u>66</u>th book concluding the bible. Then observe the numbers given to the verse, 13:18. 13 is the <u>6</u>th prime number, and 18 = <u>6+6+6</u>. The first bible to be printed on the printing press was the "Gutenberg Bible" first printed late 1455.

"New Testament" **66** RN.

"Number of a Man" **66** RN.
"Here is Wisdom" **66** N.
"Number of the Beast" **66** N.
"Mankind" **66** AO.
"Gutenberg Bible" **66** N.
Genesis **6:6**
"Revelation" 121 AO.
"Apocalyptic" 121 AO.
121= 11^2. (1+2+3+4+5+6+7+8+9+10+11= **66**.) Thus **66** is the 11th Triangular Number.

Revelation 13:18 ESV
"This calls for *wisdom*: let the one who has understanding calculate the number of the beast, for it is the number of a man, and his number is **666**."
   To make a modern day comparison at this point, lets consider how many are looking at 2020 as a year filled with "apocalypse" events. And don't forget who was president at the start of the year, the orange Trump with the slogan "Make America Great Again". The title of 'Maga' is attributed to a 5th degree member of the Satanic Church~ *www.churchofsatan.com/hierarchy/.* Reminding of the story in Revelation about the trumpets that will signal the beginning of the apocalypse. Now laugh at the "TrumpPence" ticket, whose supporters went around wearing MAGA gear.

"Make American Great Again" 404 RAO.

"This calls for wisdom: let the one who has understanding calculate the number of the beast," 404 RN.
"And It Grieved Him To His Heart." 404 RAO.
Genesis **6:6** ESV
"And the LORD regretted that He had made man on the earth, and it grieved Him to His heart"

   What is the mark of the **beast** that must be on the face or hand of those who receive it in order to take part in trade? Many raised concerning parralells over the jab in the arm and mask on the face during the pandemic. Again Donald Trump made the vaccination a military operation while at the same Q-Annon psychological operations were being done. What is the only entity in our world that could enforce the taking of such a mark? ~ *Want to Enter a School Building? Get Scanned First. Edtechmagazine.com. October 14th, 2020.*
   "16 It also forced all people, great and small, rich and poor, free and slave, to receive a mark on their right hands or on their foreheads, 17 so that they could not buy or sell unless they had the mark, which is the name of the beast or the number of its name."

"A Mark" 17 N.
"Shot" 17 N.
"Beast" **47** AO.
"Government" **47** RN.

On the following page is a letter table giving the Sumerian cipher. The Sumerians based their mathematic systems around the number 6. To this day we have 60 minutes in an hour, a measurment attributed to Sumerian culture. Consider we are dealing with prophecies and that Sumerian culture is estimated to have ended, approximately 2000 B.C. If we apply their facisnation with the number 6 to the english lanuage we find some stunning 'revelations'.
~SUMERIAN/BABYLONIAN MATHEMATICS.
Storyofmathematics.com.

ENGLISH SUMERIAN (ES)

A=6	B=12	C=16	D=24	E=30	F=36
G=42	H=48	I=54	J=60	K=66	L=72
M=78	N=84	O=90	P=96	Q=102	R=108
S=114	T=120	U=126	V=132	W=138	X=144
Y=150	Z=156				

"Mandatory" **666** ES
"Vaccination" **666** ES
"Bio Implant" **666** ES
"Humanity" **666** ES
"Dollar Sign" **666** ES
"Pazuzu" **666** ES (Evil god of ancient Sumerian culture)

Humans, and all life forms on earth carry "carbon". Carbon is composed of **6** neutrons, **6** protons, and **6** electrons. To further the point carbon has an atomic number of **6**. All this riddled around "The number of man" while we are composed of carbon which has a **666** tribute in itself.

"Carbon" **26** N.
"God" **26** AO.

Another interesting connection that needs to be pointed out is the fact that **666** is the 36th triangular number (1+2+3+4+5....+35+36=**666**). 36 is also a multiple of 6.(**6×6=36**). To further this point and tie it back to the main man of the New Testament, "Jesus Christ"=*151* AO. Know that *151* is the 36th prime number. So there is this correlation with 36, *151*, and **666**, all numbers pertaining to Jesus and this New Testament riddle.

"Jesus Christ" *151* AO.

The Clade X simulation, something every American should be aware of, was hosted by the Johnson and Johnson corporation. It took place in Washington D.C. yet at the time just another passing headline of 'A Pandemic Exercise'. This event took place May 15th, 2018 with the research still available at www.centerforhealthsecurity.org. If one were to measure from the date this 'simulation' event took place, to the date the pandemic was officially declared by The World Health Organization, March 11th, 2020. Then one would see that the calculation between those dates is exactly, **666** days. ~*https://www.centerforhealthsecurity.org/our-work/exercises/2018_clade_x_exercise/..*

Relating 666 to the beginning of America's history, when the first Americans held a vote for independence it was on the date July 2nd 1776. However they had previously held The First Continental Congress on September 5th, 1774. The congress initially discussed how to respond to increasing coercive actions from the British. Notice that from September 5th 1774, the meeting of the First Continental Congress, to the date America voted for independence, July 2nd 1776 is exactly, **666** days.

Arguably the worlds most influential occultist, Alister Crowley, brought occultism into the mainstream with his multiple books and celebrity influence. With song like "Mr. Crowley" by Ozzy Osbourne, and The Beatles having him appear on their album cover for 'Sgt. Peppers Lonely Hearts Club Band'. He himself proclaimed that he was the beast after there were scandals written about him. Crowley never lacked followers and was in demand as a medium to the end of his days. He died, in Hastings, in 1947.

"Beast" **47** AO.

   Crowley used multiple pseudonyms but the most common that he referred to himself as was "θηριον" in English this is the word "Beast". If you transliterate the Greek name "θηριον" into English it would be "Theryon". If you transliterate the same Greek word "θηριον" into Hebrew it would be תריון.

תריון   **666** HG (Transliteration of "θηριον" meaning 'Beast')
"ομεγάλος θηρίο"   616 GI (The Great Beast)

   *Professor David Parker, Professor of New Testament Textual Criticism and Paleography at the University of Birmingham, thinks that 616, although less memorable than **666**, is the original. He said: "This is an example of gematria, where numbers are*

based on the numerical values of letters in people's names. Early Christians would use numbers to hide the identity of people who they were attacking: _616_ refers to the Emperor Caligula. The Book of Revelation is traditionally considered to be written by John, a disciple of Jesus; it identifies **666** as the mark of the Antichrist."
Responding coolly to the this "Revelation".
 Peter Gilmore, High Priest of the Church of Satan, based in New York, said:
"By using **666** we're using something that the Christians fear. Mind you, if they do switch to _616_ being the number of the beast then we'll start using that." ~ 616 vs. 666: Which Is the Real Number of the Beast? Escapeallthesethings.com.

 To conclude on the mystery around the deep 666 riddle one must be aware of the first beginnings of Christian persecution in Rome, under Nero Cesar. The First Persecution of the Church, took place in the year 67 A.D. under Nero, the **6**th emperor of Rome. He notoriously blamed Christianity for the "Great Fire of Rome". If we're to take the name of Nero Cesar and translate it to Hebrew it would be rendered as, נרון קסר. If we apply Hebrew Gematria below we get a stunning 'revelation' about the first man to greatly persecute the Christians.

נרון קסר   **666** HG (Nero Cesar)

Could this be a sign that the terrible **666** has already played out in history or was it another play called from the Biblical Playbook? Knowing that the religious themes hold sway over the majority, why not make your schemes symbolically align? In this way a leadership could make ideals passively accepted by those holding modern religious ideas of 'prophecy'. For those of the nihilistic stream of thought, karma is a joke as coincidence is king. If the majority of society is willing to accept their mythos as literal what then would they not believe from their government? If a society doesn't understand that within them is already the marks of a beast how then will they truly prevent it from being unleashed?

The Curious Case of Constantine- Constantine the Great is attributed as the emperor that brought Christianity to Rome. In the year 312 C.E. Constantine converted to Christianity, being the first emperor to do so. Some modern scholars allege that his main objective was to gain approval and confirmation of his authority from all classes. Choosing Christianity as his frame for propaganda, believing that it was the most appropriate religion to fit with the current Imperial cults.

In The Battle of the Milvian Bridge, there was a battle between Constantines out numbered troops and Maxentius' army. Constantine ordered his troops to paint the cross on their shields. After winning the battle it was concluded that this was divine intervention, implying Constantine was a wielder of divine forces. This divine portrayal isn't uncommon among Roman rulers of the period. Many emperors had stories written of them in mythical detail. As history has it the truth is usually more interesting that fiction. The "Arch of Constantine" depicts The Battle of the Milvain Bridge, it still survives to this day. Although the monument depicts the battle there are no carvings depicting a cross on shields or any Christian iconography. There is however the symbols of Sol Invictus, common among the Roman military. One panel shows Constantine surrounded by Roman pagan gods. *~Arch Of Constantine. employees.oneonta.edu.* This alone can shed much light on how hard Constantine was working to make himself the sole ruler of Rome, a land of vast diversity and looming civil wars. The crowning achievement of his rule he created the city of "Constantinople".

"Constantinople" **201** RAO.
"Ignatius of Loyola" **201** AO.
"The Jesuit Order" **201** RAO.
"His Resurrection" **201** AO.

"Arch of Constantine" *77* N.
"The Savior of Man" *77* RN.
"Christ" *77* AO.

"Sol Invictus" *163* AO.
"Constantine" *163* RAO.

   Just like Christians the military officers in the
Roman cult of Mithras believed in resurrection. It's
easy to see how this could be popular among military
personal who had to rush into battle on call.
Unfortunately, classical Mithraic written texts and
ancient manuscripts on Mithraicism do not exist.
However, statues of Mithra can still be found in the
remains of caves and temples. Mithra is always
shown standing over a bull, slitting its throat.
~ *"The temples of Mithras were always an*
underground cave, featuring a relief of Mithras
killing the bull. This "tauroctony", as it is known
today, appears in the same format everywhere, but
with minor variations. Other standard themes
appear in the iconography."tertullian.org. The
Zodiac sign of Taurus is strongly associated with a
bull. People born under Taurus are usually adept
with their coordination and development of their
bodies. The bull is associated with the psychical
body or lower, animal nature in man. ~ *"There's no*
zodiac sign that's more in tune with their physical
senses (and their tangible pleasures) than a Taurus.
Taureans can easily get lost in the sensations of a
loving massage, a gourmet meal, a bouquet of
fragrant flowers, or a powerful piece of music...".
Taurus Zodiac Sign Biggest Strengths. Bustle.com.

Thus 'slaying the bull' or 1ˢᵗ Corinthians 11:23-24 ESV "The Lord Jesus on the night when he was betrayed took bread, and when he had given thanks, <u>he broke it</u>, and said, "**This is my body**, which is for you. Do this in remembrance of me."
"The word became flesh"

"Mithra' *93* RAO.
"Crucifix" *93* AO.
"God's Son" *93* AO.
"Solar Man" *93* AO.

With Sol Invictus appearing on so many coins during his reign it seemed clear that Constantine had identified him as the "Highest Divinity". *Curator's comments- "Constantine is shown and described as the 'companion' of the sun god on a coin minted nearly four years after his reported conversion to Christianity on the eve of the battle of the Milvain Bridge. The emperor copies Sol's characteristic gesture of benediction seen on the most common coins (copper alloy nummi) of Constantine until AD 317 (and occasionally on the gold into the 320s). It is possible that the Milvian Bridge conversion was a suitably dramatic fiction given out long afterwards, but a Christian of the time would have regarded the figure as nothing more than a representation of the weekly holy day of Sunday (dies Solis). Sunday was made an official day of rest for all by Constantine in*

AD 321." ~
*https://www.britishmuseum.org/collection/object/C_*
1863-0713-1.

   One relic built in Constantinople was the Column of Constantine. In Constantine's day the column was at the center of the Forum of Constantine. On its erection, the top of the column was mounted by a statue of Constantine in the archetypal pose of Apollo. At the foot of the column was a sanctuary which contained relics, allegedly, from the crosses of the two <u>con</u>victs who were crucified with Jesus, the baskets from the loaves and fishes miracle, an alabaster ointment jar belonging to Mary Magdalene that was used by her for anointing the head and feet of Jesus. In light of all the spiritual propaganda employed by Constantine, where do you think the English prefix 'Con', gets its meaning?

"Apollo" 71 AO.
"Sol Invictus" 71 RN.

As is the modern western tradition I have insensitively started with the stories of Jesus and will now go back to cover the Old Testament. A story of the Jewish nation and their journey as 'God's chosen people'.

Deuteronomy 14:2 ESV

For you are a holy people to the Lord your God, and the Lord has chosen you to be a people for His own possession out of all the peoples who are on the face of the earth.

TANAKH תַּנַ״ךְ - We know that in Hebrew, letters and numbers were intended to be interchangeable. We covered how there is much encoded in the English rendering of the bible. To what extent is there overlap between Hebrew and English Gematria values? While there is undoubtedly more to be discovered here are a few examples to ponder:

Know when reading Hebrew you read from right to left and traditionally vowels are not written in the text. There is also multiple names attributed to 'God' unlike in English where "God" or sometimes "Lord" are basically the only names attributed. Another concept to be aware of is that some Jews will render God as, G'd. The belief being that if you were to write 'God' on a piece of paper you would have to treat that piece of paper as now being Holy. So to get around this they render it as G'd. G=7 ' D=4. **7'4.**

"Jewish" **74** AO.
"Gematria" **74** AO.

It is interesting that the Tanakh is constantly insinuating "and God said", "Thus says the Lord", "and God spoke" etc. something that is surprisingly not often claimed in the New Testament although I will concede many renditions put Jesus words in red to signify his authority. However, it is still debated among christian sects if Jesus was divine and part of a trinity, if he was God in human form, or an 'avatar' God used.

Numbers 23:19 ESV

"God is not man, that he should lie, or a son of man, that he should change his mind."

"Jews" *57* AO.
"And God Said" *57* RN.
"Wine" *57* RAO
"The Key To Life" *57* RN.
"Moon" *57* AO.
The Jews follow the Lunar Calendar.

On the topic of *57* and the Jews lets look at one of the key verses that Jews use to deny the divinity of Jesus. Being that they were one of if not the first to promote the idea of "mono" theism.

Deuteronomy *5:7* ESV

"You shall have no other gods before me."

"Mono" *57* AO.
"False Prophet" *57* RN.
"Mosaic Code" *57* RN.

What does Christianity say about the God of this earth?

2nd Corinthians 4:3-4 ESV

"And even if our gospel is veiled, it is veiled to those who are perishing. 4 In their case the god of this world has blinded the minds of unbelievers, to keep them from seeing the light of the gospel of the glory of <u>Christ, who is the image of God</u>."

"God Is Not A Man, That He Should Lie" **<u>430</u>** RAO.
"Jesus Christ" **43** N.
"No other gods before me" *<u>304</u>* RAO.
"Jesus" *34* RN.

"<u>Even If Our Gospel Is Veiled</u>" **121** N. <u>122</u> RN.
"Thirty Third Degree Mason" **121** N. <u>122</u> RN.
"Solar Cult" **121** AO. <u>122</u> RAO.
"IESUS HOMINUM SALVATOR" <u>122</u> RN.

In "The Old Testament" there are a total of *55* prophets, **48** males and *7* females, with a total of *17* books of prophecies. Interestingly enough the suffix "Fe" sums to *7* for the *7* Female prophets and *17* is the *7ᵗʰ* prime number. With 17 and 55 being values of "God".

"Fe" *7* RN.
"God" *17* N. *55* RAO
"The Old Testament" *55* N.
"Tanakh" *55* AO. *107* RAO.

One who spoke for God in antiquity was often referred to as "an Oracle" or "the Oracle" which is defined as "God's speaker". Most of the prophecies received came in the form of dreams or while in a "mystical trance".

"God" *55* RAO.
"Mystical Trance" *55* N.
"A Oracle" *55* AO.
48 Male Prophets
"An Oracle" **48** RN.
"The Oracle" **48** RN.
"God's Speaker" **48** N.
To Receive" **48** N.
"Manifest" **48** RN.
גדולה   **48** HG (Greatness, Majesty, Renown)
חיל   **48** HG (Force, Power, Might)

"In the beginning God created" **123** RN
"In the beginning was the word" **123** RN

1,2,3

בְּרֵאשִׁית בָּרָא אֱלֹהִים אֵת הַשָּׁמַיִם וְאֵת הָאָרֶץ Genesis 1:1
"In the beginning of God's creation of the heavens and the earth,"

   We should look closely at the context being set with the first Hebrew word בְּרֵאשִׁית meaning "at the head". Next we should look at the last letters of the next three words. Doing so renders the Hebrew word אמת meaning "truth". Thus the Hebrew bible could be interpreted as stating "In the beginning, there was Truth. Adding up the first Hebrew letter in each word equals 22, the amount of letters in the Hebrew alphabet.

$$בְּ + בָּ + אֱ + אֵ + הַ + וְ + הָ = 22$$

Genesis 1:26
ויאמר אלהים נעשה אדם בצלמנו כדמותנו וירדו בדגת הים ובעוף השמים ובבהמה ובכל־הארץ ובכל־הרמש הרמש על־הארץ

Genesis 1:**26** ESV
And God said, let us make man in our image, after our likeness, and let them go down in the fish of the sea, and in the fowl of the air, and in the beast, and in all the earth, and in every creeping thing that creeps upon the earth."

יהוה   **26** HG

"God" **26** AO.

"Adam" **26** RN.

"Image" **26** N.

"Sixth" **26** N.

"Torah" **26** N.

חבוי   26 HG (Hidden)

The adult human skeleton is composed of **206** bones.

"Bones" **26** RN.

"Skeleton" 101 AO. 101 the 26th Prime Number in sequence of Primes.

"Make man in our image" *170* AO. 100 RN.

"God" *17* N. 10 RN.

"Man" 10 N. *17* RN.

In the practice of Gematria it is conveyed the way God created the world through language, mathematics, and sound. The number **6**, being the first perfect number, representing perfection, and the number **8** representing infinite. Mankind, the grand symbol of perfection made on the **6**th day. Up until God makes Adam in Genesis 1:<u>26</u> the Bible quotes **"God said" 8 times**, think of how the ancients believed there were 7 planets; 1.Moon, 2.Mercury, 3.Venus, 4.Sun, 5.Mars, 6.Jupiter, and 7.Saturn. The earth finished in its creation after the **8** statements, being the **8**th planet.

"The Vesica Piscis" **68** N.
"The Eye" **68** AO.
"Sacred Geometry" **68** N.
"Mathematics" **68** RN.
"Language" **68** AO.
"Old Testament" **68** RN.
"Planet" **68** AO.
"The Holy Spirit" **68** RN.
חיים   **68** HG (Life)

The first letter of the Aleph-Bet is א, (Aleph). This symbol can help convey much understanding of creation. We see that the letter is itself actually a combination of two other letters, י the Yod and, ו the Vav. Both being letters that are used in the sacred 4 letter name. Yod is like a "flame" and being the first

letter in the sacred name, think how fire is used to symbolize the "spirit" in all religions. Separating the symbol into its parts reveals something of a percent sign. Showing the balance of two poles on either side or the Lower world mirroring the Higher world. Interestingly, the Hebrew word אחד, meaning '1' or 'single', has a value of 13, the holy name balanced or halved. Yod has the numerical value of 10, and Vav has the value of 6. Thus Aleph in the sum of it's parts is <u>26.</u>
(יYod + וVav + יYod) or (10 + 6 + 10= <u>26</u>).
 The same parable above holds true in the symbolism of a checkerboard. 32+ white squares, 32- black squares, as there are 32 Paths to either polarity on The Tree of Life (pg. 239). The Aleph symbol can also be seen as the spiral of the milky way ever expanding or The Word echoing throughout all space.

"Magnetism" 101 AO.
101 the <u>26</u>[th] Prime Number in sequence of Primes
"Polar" <u>26</u> N.

אחד   **13** HG (Singular) (One)
אהבה   **13** HG (Love)
"Soul" **13** N.
"Flame" 37 RAO.
"Spirit" 37 N.

‎צ‎
%
‎א‎

Genesis *2:7* KJV

"And the LORD God formed man *of* the dust of the ground, and breathed into his nostrils the breath of life; and man became a living soul."

"Breath" *27* N.

"Dust" **26** RN.

"Soil" **26** RN.

"Air" **26** RN.

"Formed" 101 RAO. 101 the 26th Prime Number in sequence of Primes.

The Hebrew word for 'growth', גדילה , has the value of **52**. Like the Earth we inhabit grows throughout a **52** week period. Not unrelated is the **52**nd mitzvot, Deuteronomy 16:21 ESV

"You shall not GROW for yourself an asherah, or any tree, near the altar of the Lord, your God, which you shall make for yourself."

"Earth" **52** AO.

גדילה   **52** HG (Growth)

Genesis 1:**29** KJV

"And God said, Behold, I have given you every herb bearing seed, which *is* upon the face of all the earth, and every tree, in the which *is* the fruit of a tree yielding seed; to you it shall be for meat."

"Earth" *83* RAO. **29** RN.
"Ground" *79* AO. *34* N. *83* RAO. **29** RN.
"Seeds" *83* RAO. **29** RN.
"Flower" *79* AO. *34* N. *83* RAO. **29** RN.
"Fruit" **29** N. *34* RN.

In light of God breathing the breath of life into the man made of the dust of the ground, observe,

"Breathe the breath of life" **109** N.
109 is the **29**[th] Prime in sequence of Prime Numbers.
"Ground" **29** RN.

Genesis **2:9** KJV
"And out of the **ground** made the LORD God to grow every tree that is pleasant to the sight, and good for food; the tree of life also in the midst of the garden, and the tree of knowledge of good and evil."

"Twenty Nine" **50** N.
"Creation" **50** RN.
"Biblical" **50** AO.

When presented with the story of Cain and Abel the meaning appears to be very on the surface. However when carefully reading one can get interesting insights. Genesis **4:7** sees the beginning of the downfall of Cain.
Genesis **4:7** KJV

"If thou doest well, shalt thou not be accepted? and if thou doest not well, sin lieth at the door. And unto thee shall be his desire, and thou shalt rule over him."

The key information to note is God saying you must rule over sin. Notice he doesn't state "I will provide a 'savior' as a sacrifice for you and the rest of the worlds 'sin'" but rather puts the responsibility on the individual.

"Thou Shalt Rule Over Him." *270* AO. *270* RAO.
"Cain" *27* AO. *27* RN.

"Mankind's Sins" **47** N.
"Beast" **47** AO.
"Sins" **47** RAO.
Genesis **4:7**

"Individual Responsibility" 351 RAO.
351 Is the 26th Triangular Number in sequence,
"God" 26 AO.

Genesis 4:8-10 KJV
And Cain talked with Abel his brother: and it came to pass, when they were in the field, that Cain rose up against Abel his brother, and slew him. 9 And the LORD said unto Cain, Where is Abel thy brother? And he said, I know not: Am I my brother's keeper

10 And he said, What hast thou done? the voice of thy brother's blood crieth unto me from the ground.

   Cain is punished by God and he receives "a mark" in 4:15.

Genesis 4:15 KJV

"And the Lord said unto him, Therefore whosoever slayeth Cain, vengeance shall be taken on him *sevenfold*. And the Lord set a mark upon Cain, lest any finding him should kill him."

"A Mark" **44** AO. 17 N.

"Kill" **44** AO. 17 N. *28* RN.

"Am I My Brother's Keeper" 107 RN.

107 is the *28th* Prime in sequence of Prime Numbers, relating to the word "kill".

Genesis 4:23-24 KJV

Lamech said to his wives, "Adah and Zillah, listen to me; wives of Lamech, hear my words. I have killed a man for wounding me, a young man for injuring me. 24 If Cain is avenged *seven times*, then Lamech *seventy-seven times*."

   Here we see that the Tanakh is talking about forces being multiplied for the act of seeking revenge. If you multiply the 7 x curse put on Cain by the 77 x curse put on Lamech you arrive at 7×77= 539. If you then add (5 + 3 + 9= 17). With these forces being multiplied for seeking revenge, let us seek insight at the opposite pole. In Luke chapter 17 we are given instructions on "forgiveness".

Luke 17:4 ESV

"Even if they sin against you *seven times* in a day and *seven times* come back to you saying 'I repent' you must forgive them."

The bible instructs us to seek forgiveness and not take retribution into our own hands. This is because "God" is in control of the forces of "Karma". To seek revenge by ones own judgments and schemes is to deny the natural enforcement of karmic forces set in place by God.

"Kill" 44 AO. 17 N.
"Karma" 44 AO. 17 N.
"Am I My Brother's Keeper" 107 RN.
"God" 17 N.
"Forgiveness" 59 RN.
59 is the 17th Prime Number

An eye for an eye is seemingly one of the oldest human concepts. Even today, children who get prodded or pushed aside by other children will instinctually respond by returning the same amount of force. Those with experience in martial arts, yoga, or tai chi, are aware of the concept of controlling this push and pull of force. The great 1965 Oklahoma State Wrestling All American, Russ Winer, explained this concept to me as 'kinetic energy', saying: 'You should be able to close your eyes and visualize the amount and force of energy that is being distributed between you and your opponent while you are wrestling.'. Russ Winer went on to be inducted into National and State Hall of Fames as a coach, having a *69.9%* career winning coaching record over 26+ years.~ *azcoachhof.org*. 'For every action there is an equal and opposite reaction.' - Issac Newton

Genesis **9:6**
שפך דם האדם באדם דמו ישפך כי בצלם אלהים עשה את־האדם
Genesis **9:6** ESV
"Whoever sheds the blood of man, by man shall his blood be shed, for God made man in his own image."

"Whoever Shed The Blood" **96** N.
"First Degree Murder" **96** N.

"Laws Of Karma" *69* RN.
"Winer" *69* AO.
Genesis *6:9* ESV
Noah was a righteous man, blameless in his generation.

   From Genesis chapters 6-9 is the story of the "flood" of the "earth". In the year 19**52** weather weapons were first admitted to by the Royal Air Force, who in their attempt to increase rainfall caused a flood. Which reminds of the last mass flooding in Texas from Hurricane Harvey on August 29th 2017. August 29th is the 239th day of the year, and 239 is the **52nd** prime number.

"Flood" **52** AO. **25** N. *83* RAO.
"Earth" **52** AO. **25** N. *83* RAO.
Genesis *8:3* ESV
"and the waters receded from the earth continually. At the end of 150 days the waters had abated."

In Genesis 30:23-24 we get the first mention of Joseph, who's name in Hebrew would be pronounced "Yosef". His name is given to him by Rachel who is thankful to God after she was unable to conceive a child.
Genesis 30:23-24 KJV
"And she conceived, and bare a son; and said, God hath taken away my reproach: 24 And she called his name Joseph; and said, The LORD shall add to me another son."

Chapter 30+ Verse 23= **53**
"Son of Rachel" **53** N.
"Son of Jacob" **53** RN

Later Joseph's brothers become jealous of him and abandon him into slavery after he explains his dreams to them and their father continues to favor him. After all this Joseph guided by God is able to be a "dream interpreter" to the Pharaoh, who grants him the title of "vizier".

Genesis 37:3-4 KJV

"Now Israel loved Joseph more than all his children, because he was the son of his old age: and he made him a coat of many colours." Be aware that some contest it was not a coat with many colors but some translations render it as a "coat with long sleeves"

"Son of Jacob" 37 N.
"Dreamer" 37 N. 44 RN.
"Vizier" 44 N. 37 RN.

"Ten Half Brothers" 234 RAO. 81 RN. (The coat with long sleeves is what made his brothers jealous)
"Coat with long sleeves" 234 AO. 81 N. 99 RN.
"Dream Interpreter" 99 RN.
"Zaphenath" 99 AO.

Genesis 41: 41-42 KJV

"41 So Pharaoh said to Joseph, "I hereby put you in charge of the whole land of Egypt." 42 Then Pharaoh took his signet ring from his finger and put it on Joseph's finger. He dressed him in robes of fine linen and put a gold chain around his neck."
"Pharaoh's Dream" 71 RN.
"Yosef" 20 RN.
71 is the 20th Prime in sequence of Prime Numbers.

The name "Yosef" literally translates as "to increase" and the title Zaphenath-Paneah which translates literally as "a revealer of secrets"

"To increase" **109** AO.
"A revealer of secrets" **109** RN.

Let us now research the synchronicity involving the most high prophet in the Old Testament "Moses".

"Moses" **17** N.
"God" **17** N.
"The Lord" **107** RAO.
"A Staff" **17** N.
"Rod" **17** RN.
"Parting the Red Sea" **170** AO.
"Egypt" **17** RN.

"Pharaoh of Egypt" *161* AO. *217* RAO.
"A Mass Departure" *161* AO. *217* RAO. (The literal meaning of Exodus)

"Exodus" <u>88</u> AO. <u>25</u> N.
"Black Slave" <u>88</u> AO. <u>25</u> N.

In light of the strong **17** connection lets skim through chapter 1-4 only viewing the **17**th verse in each.
Exodus 1:**17** KJV

"But the midwives feared God, and did not as the king of Egypt commanded them, but saved the men children alive. "
Exodus 2:**17** KJV
"And the shepherds came and drove them away: but Moses stood up and helped them, and watered their flock."
Exodus 3:**17** KJV
"And I have said, I will bring you up out of the affliction of Egypt unto the land of the Canaanites, and the Hittites, and the Amorites, and the Perizzites, and the Hivites, and the Jebusites, unto a land flowing with milk and honey."
Exodus 4:**17** KJV
"And thou shalt take this rod in thine hand, wherewith thou shalt do signs."
Exodus 4:**17** ESV "And take in your hand this staff, with which you shall do the signs."

Before Moses is presented with the 10 commandments and gives us the "Mosaic Code" he first had to bring his fellow Jews out of "slavery". To prove that they were "God's people" there were "Ten plagues" sent to Egypt to twist their arm into releasing them. While they were enslaved they were forced to build the city of "Pithom". God gives Moses the rod to "perform miracles" with which resulted in jews "Crossing the Red Sea" and escaping from "Ramesses".

"Mosaic Code" <u>87</u> AO. <u>42</u> N.
"Slavery" <u>87</u> RAO. <u>42</u> RN.

"God's People" *51* N. *39* RN.
"Ten Plagues" *39* N. *51* RN.

"Perform Miracles" **81** N.
"Pithom" **81** AO. **81** RAO. *27* RN.
"Crossing the Red Sea" **81** N. *270* RAO. <u>99</u> RN.
"Ramesses" <u>99</u> AO. *27* N.

In the Hebrew bible and manifest in the culture are
many tributes to the number **70**. Wine, "יין", is often
associated with Jewish tradition and used
symbolically throughout the bible. Relating to this,
in the Kiddush prayer there are **70** words.
Deuteronomy 10:22 "Your ancestors who went down
into Egypt were **seventy** in all, and now the LORD
your God has made you as numerous as the stars in
the sky." After escaping from Egypt Moses appoints
70 elders in Numbers 11: 16 "Then the LORD said
to Moses, "Gather for me **seventy** men of the elders
of Israel, whom you know to be the elders of the
people and officers over them, and bring them to the
tent of meeting, and let them take their stand there
with you." The Sanhedrin was traditionally
composed of **70** sages from the various tribes. The
Babylonian exile was told to last for **70** years in
Jeremiah 25: 12. "But when the **seventy** years are

fulfilled, I will punish the king of Babylon and his nation, the land of the Babylonians, for their guilt," declares the Lord, "and will make it desolate forever."

The Hebrew word for 'secret' is rendered as "סוד", it also last in the acronym P.R.D.S.
In which the S stands for, סוד, Sod the deepest or mystical part of biblical texts.
P- Pershat- Historical or literal
R- Remez- Allegorical
D- Drash- Moral or Implementable
S- Sod- Secret, Concealed, or Mystical

סוד	**70** HG (Secret)
יין	**70** HG (Wine)

"Cover Your Eyes" **70** N.
"Star of David" **70** RN.

When you say שְׁמַע, it is proper to "cover your eyes" so that one may "visualize" the "Holy Spirit". The "Shema" can be recited as soon as one "awakens" to show graciousness. This can be gleamed from Deuteronomy *6:7*, which synchronizes well being that *67* is the **19**th prime number.

Deuteronomy *6:7* ESV
You shall teach them diligently to your children, and shall talk of them when you sit in your house, and when you walk by the way, and when you lie down, and when you rise.

"Shema" **19** N.
"Awaken" **19** N.
"None good but <u>one</u>" **67** N. (**67** the **19**th Prime Number, quote from Mathew chapter **19**) (pg. 73).

שְׁמַע יִשְׂרָאֵל יְהוָה אֱלֹהֵינוּ יְהוָה אֶחָד
Hear, O Israel: The Lord our God, the Lord is <u>one</u>.

"All Seeing Eye" **119** AO. 56 N.
"Visualize" **119** RAO. 56 RN.
"The Spirit" **119** RAO. 56 RN.
"Holy Spirit" **119** RAO. 56 RN.
"Four Worlds" **119** RAO. 56 RN.
"Star of David" **119** AO.

There are **187** chapters in Torah. The Torah is the essential base for all three of the 'Abrahamic' religions. This includes Judaism, Christianity, and Islam.
"And God said, Let there be light, and there was light. And God saw that the light was good. And God separated the light from the darkness."
<u>1117</u> AO. *487* N.
487 is the *93*rd Prime Number.
"The Word" *93* AO.
<u>1117</u> is the **187**th Prime Number.
"Abrahamic" **187** RAO.
"All God's Prophets" **187** AO.
"Dreams of Prophecy" **187** AO.

One can also find 'Fibonacci' concepts in the Hebrew bible. Both 144 and 233 are Fibonacci numbers that follow each other in sequence. Observe how the Hebrew word for 'Garden of Eden' קדם has the numerical value of 144. Note 144 is the 12th number in the sequence of Fibonacci. This is very interesting to note, because of all the 12 symbolism that is to play out as consequence of the trials in Eden, not to mention the 12 pairs of cranial nerves the concept of the garden is rooted in. Also that 144 is 12^2 corresponding the 12 Pairs of nerves. 'Tree of Life' עץ החיים has the value of 233, the 13th number in the sequence. 13 is a number relating to "kundalini", a spiritual practice focusing on spiritual ascension up the spine. There is an average of 13 million neurons in the human spine. In the longest region of the spine there are 12 thoracic vertebrae, where man's larynx sits atop. The larynx, commonly called the voice box, is an organ in the top of the neck involved in breathing, producing sound and vibrations. This connection is most interesting when considered in light of 13 symbolism and man's future evolution.

עץ החיים   **233** HG
"Philosophers stone" **233** AO.
"Mystery Religions" **233** AO.

If someone is suffering from a type of 'nocturnal pollution' the rabbis recommend reading 10 תהלים (Psalm). This is because the numerical value for תהלים is corresponding to לְיִלִיתה the name of the evil spirit appointed over the קליפ (Klipot). It is recommended in Hebrew philosophy to never say this name out loud.

| תהלים | 485 HG (Psalms) |
| לְיִלִיתה | 485 HG |

There are a total of **613** commandments in the Torah, 248 positive and *365* negative. The Sages taught that the 248 positive commandments correspond to what man can do with his 248 bones and joints, excluding the teeth. The *365* negative commandments correspond the *365* tendons pulling man into action. Negative can be associated with the word 'passive' and there is no requirement in Judaism to preform the negative commandments precisely because they are to be passively obeyed. This corresponds to the solar year of *365* days, in which mankind is passively subject to the rays of the Sun. The phrase **המאררים** means, 'to cause a curse', and is used in Numbers 5:18.

Numbers 5:18

העמיד הכהן את־האשה לפני יהוה ופרע את־ראש האשה ונתן על־כפיה את מנחת הזכרון מנחת קנאת הוא וביד הכהן יהיו מי המרים **המאררים**

Numbers 5:18 ESV
"And the priest shall set the woman before the Lord and unbind the hair of the woman's head and place in her hands the grain offering of remembrance, which is the grain offering of jealousy. And in his hand the priest shall have the water of bitterness **that brings the curse**."

המאררים 496 HG (To cause a curse)

248 + 248= **496**.

248 positive commandments.

This is to convey the point, numerically, that the one committing adultery is to cause a curse on the 248 bones of themselves and their lover. Listed below is how the Sages came to this total:

מָאתַיִם וְאַרְבָּעִים וּשְׁמֹנָה אֵבָרִים בָּאָדָם, שְׁלֹשִׁים בְּפִסַּת הָרֶגֶל, שִׁשָּׁה בְּכָל אֶצְבַּע, עֲשָׂרָה בַּקַּרְסֹל, שְׁנַיִם בַּשּׁוֹק, חֲמִשָּׁה בָּאַרְכֻּבָּה, אֶחָד בַּיָּרֵךְ, שְׁלֹשָׁה בַּקַּטְלִית, אַחַת עֶשְׂרֵה צְלָעוֹת, שְׁלֹשִׁים בְּפִסַּת הַיָּד, שִׁשָּׁה בְּכָל אֶצְבַּע, שְׁנַיִם בַּקָּנֶה, וּשְׁנַיִם בַּמַּרְפֵּק, אֶחָד בַּזְּרוֹעַ, וְאַרְבָּעָה בַּכָּתֵף. מֵאָה וְאֶחָד מִזֶּה וּמֵאָה וְאֶחָד מִזֶּה. וּשְׁמֹנָה עֶשְׂרֵה חֻלְיוֹת בַּשִּׁדְרָה, תִּשְׁעָה בָּרֹאשׁ, שְׁמֹנָה בַּצַּוָּאר, שִׁשָּׁה בַּמַּפְתֵּחַ שֶׁל לֵב, וַחֲמִשָּׁה בִנְקָבָיו. כָּל אֶחָד וְאֶחָד מְטַמֵּא בְמַגָּע וּבְמַשָּׂא וּבְאֹהֶל. אֵימָתַי, בִּזְמַן שֶׁיֵּשׁ עֲלֵיהֶן בָּשָׂר כָּרָאוּי. אֲבָל אִם אֵין עֲלֵיהֶן בָּשָׂר כָּרָאוּי, מְטַמְּאִין בְּמַגָּע וּבְמַשָּׂא, וְאֵין מְטַמְּאִין בְּאֹהֶל

There are two hundred and forty-eight limbs in a human body: Thirty in the foot, six for every toe, Ten in the ankle, Two in the shin, Five in the knee, One in the thigh, Three in the hip, Eleven ribs, Thirty in the hand, [that is] six to every finger, Two in the fore-arm, Two in the elbow, One in the upper arm and Four in the shoulder, [For a total of] one hundred and one on the one side [of the body] and one hundred and one on the other. Eighteen vertebrae in the spine, Nine in the head, Eight in the neck, Six in the key of the heart, And five around the genitals. Each one [of these] can defile by contact, carriage or overshadowing. When is this so? When they have upon them the appropriate amount of flesh, But if they do not have the appropriate amount flesh upon them, they can defile by contact and carriage but cannot defile by overshadowing.
~ *Mishnah Oholot 1:8. Sefaria.org.*

30 in the foot — 6 in each toe
10 in the ankle
2 in the shin
5 in the knee
1 in the thigh
3 in the pelvis
11 ribs
30 in the hand — 6 in each finger
2 in the forearm
2 in the elbow

1 in the upper arm
4 in the shoulder

A total of 202. 101 on the left side and 101 on the right. In the center of the human body there are the following bones:

18 vertebrae in the spine
9 in the head
8 in the neck
6 in the opening to the heart
5 in the organs of birth
=248

Now then, why did God add the letter 'H' to Abraham's name? One explanation can be made through the English language, that is, H is the first letter in 'Humanity' the name we have given ourselves. Corresponding to Abraham being the first "chosen" by God. The more biblically conclusive answer, however would go back the 248 bones and joints in the Human. Also notice this information comes in Genesis *18:18* and the Mishnah on the topic comes from Oholot *1:8*.

Genesis 18:18
אַבְרָהָם הָיוֹ יִהְיֶה לְגוֹי גָּדוֹל וְעָצוּם וְנִבְרְכוּ בוֹ כֹּל גּוֹיֵי הָאָרֶץ

Genesis 18:18 ESV
"seeing that **Abraham** shall surely become a great and mighty nation, and all the nations of the earth shall be blessed in him"

אברהם   <u>248</u> HG (Avraham)

יהוה   26 HG (YHVH)
"Abraham" 26 N.
"Chosen" 26 RN.
"God" 26 AO.

   One verse that shined brighter than ever during the Covid pandemic can be found in the ancient Hebrew scriptures. Many people were swayed by their favorite celebrities and politicians to take part in a medical experiment and receive a rapidly developed vaccine. In a times of a hostile social climate, as the public drowns in waves of propaganda, it is beneficial to find peace in The Temple.

Exodus 15:26
ויאמר אם־שמוע תשמע לקול | <u>יהוה אלהיך והישר</u> בעיניו תעשה
והאזנת למצותיו ושמרת כל־חקיו כל־המחלה אשר־שמתי
במצרים לא־אשים עליך כי **אני יהוה רפאך**

Exodus 15:26 ESV
saying, "*If you will diligently listen to the voice* of <u>the Lord your God</u>, and do that which is right in his

eyes, and give ear to his commandments and keep all his statutes, I will put none of the diseases on you that I put on the Egyptians, for **I am the Lord, your healer."**

יהוה אלהיך והישר   613 HG
(YHVH your 'righteousness')
613 Commandments in the Hebrew Bible

אני יהוה רפאך   **388** HG
(I'm your YHVH and healer)
"Transcendental Meditation" **388** RAO.
"If you will diligently listen to the voice" *450* AO.
"Holy Bible" *45* N. *45* RN.

Hebrew Culture- What is the nature of the relationship between thought, mathematics, and the Hebrew language? And of what importance is it? As discussed earlier there are 32 paths on the Tree of Life. As there are 22 letters (consonants) and 10 annotations (vowels). All things are composed of one true substance or source but have a different combination of energies from this source. These are the 10 vowels of the Hebrew system corresponding to the 10 spheres or relating to string theory, the leading physics model that displays the universe operating in 10 dimensions.

Through the Hebrew language we find a pure attempt to name everything in it's essence or spiritual name. In English we have the 7 vowels corresponding with the 7 life centers in the body. However with only life centers or vowels, there is no *body* no *consonants* to make the word. A string of vowels won't make sense in any language yet when clothed in the consonants, the vowels or life centers take on numerous expressions. "God created His Universe by the three forms of expression: Numbers, Letters, and Words."

By identifying things in patterns we come to anticipate what may yet come. Many scientists conclude this is why man has dreams. As discussed its curious how many prophecies of Tanakh came through dreams as a medium. One problem to ponder is if an individual had these 'Godly insights' or "words from God", was it received or inherently realized? Did God come down to man in his dreams or were the forms and shapes of life that man observed throughout creation subconsciously realized in these 'prophecies'?

"God"   **55** RAO.
"Tanakh" **55** AO.
כלה   **55** HG (Bride) (*Mother* Nature)
הכל   **55** HG (Everything) or (All)

הכל אמת   <u>496</u> HG (All Is Truth)

מלכות   <u>496</u> HG (Kingdom or Realm. The 10th sphere on the Tree of Life.)

אֱלֹהִים   *86* HG (Elohim), (God), or (Planet)

הטבע   *86* HG (Nature) or (Wilderness)

The sage seeks to help answer all of mans eternal questions. However simple or complex one must be rooted in truth when seeking to guide others. As it has been stated all thought and thus questions, arise through our understanding of language. A "Sage" understands the energies at play in "Life" through the understanding of the *22* letters. Thus, when asked "מהטובו", (what is good?) the "חכם" (sage) responds "חיים" (life).

חיים   <u>68</u> HG (Life)

חכם   <u>68</u> HG (Sage)

מה טובו   <u>68</u> HG (What Is Good)

"Life, it is Good" <u>68</u> RN.

"Sage" *32* AO. *76* RAO. **22** RN.

"Life" *32* AO. *76* RO. **22** RN.

"Everything is Good" **202** AO.

· People throughout the ages have complained how can there be a God when so many people have to "suffer"? The Christian understanding blames all this on original sin and the Satan figure. While the Jewish philosophy of monotheism is forced to deny this obvious dualism. The explanation for such pains and trials can be explained through the allegorical understanding of nature. Look to the "diamond", the earth's hardest natural material. The diamond is only formed out of the massive pressure it has faced from two "opposing" forces. It is our level of "awareness" and ability to notice opportunity that turns a negative situation into a positive "blessing".

"Suffer" 33 RN.
"Refine" 33 RN.
"Diamond" 33 N.
"Opposing" 33 RN.
"Blessing" 33 N.
"Awareness" 33 N.

Geometry is held sacred throughout all cultures because of its implications. The Lubavitcher Rebbe, Menachem Mendel Schneerson stated in a letter: "Geometry has the characteristics of an exact science as well as of an applied science. The same is true of our holy Torah (lehavdil ad infinitum). For though the Torah is the wisdom of G'd, the ultimate in truth and exactitude, and "no man can know its worth... and it is hidden from the eyes of all living, nevertheless, as its name, Torah (from the word hora'ah, "instruction"), implies, its purpose is to instruct our daily lives in this physical and material world."~ *Torah and Geometry. Chabad.org.*

The average distance between the Earth and the Sun is **108** times the Sun's diameter. The average distance of the Earth to the Moon is 238,800 miles, about **108** times the Moon's diameter. This makes it so the Moon appears to be the same size as the Sun during eclipses.

"Geometry" **108** AO. 45 N. **108** RAO.
""Heliocentric Universe" **108** N.
"HaShem" 54 AO. **108** RAO.
"The Mysteries Of The Zohar" **108** RN.
"Good and Evil" **108** AO. 54 N. 54 RN.

In the field of Sacred Geometry the Flower of Life is held sacred because of how many other geometric shapes can be made out of it, or factor into it, so to speak. Nearly all religions throughout the world pay homage to this symbol. Note the Flower of Life, is composed of **61**-circles, a very special amount, being the 18th Prime Number. The Flower of Life is meant to symbolize creation. Out of the many shapes that can be derived from the Flower of Life, are the "Fruit" of Life, and "the Seed of Life". It is because so many figures come from this shape, the word 'prime' equates to **61** as, God is The Prime Initiator. The symbolism within prime numbers is strength and coordination, because they cannot be divided.

"Fruit" **61** RAO.

"The Seed of Life" **61** RN.
"Prime" **61** AO.
"Dios" **61** RAO.(Spanish for "God")
"Miracle" **61** AO.
"Holy Spirit" **61** N.
"Christian" **61** RN.
"Jesus" **61** RAO.
"Church" **61** AO.

"The Prime Initiator" *101* RAO.
101 is the *26th* Prime in sequence of Primes.
"God" *26*

It isn't common to see a young man at his bar mitzvah receive gifts coming in increments of $**18**. In American culture, **18** is when people are legally considered adults. **R** is the **18th** letter in the English alphabet and you must pass as an adult to enter an **R** rated movie. The Hebrew word זֹהַר (Zohar) is often translated to English as '**R**adiance'. It was not permitted to enter "the mysteries of the Zohar" until one had proven their maturity. The Hebrew word חי (Hki) translates to English as 'life'.

חי   **18** HG (Life)
61 is the **18th** Prime Number in sequence of Primes.
"The Seed of Life" **61** RN.
"Miracle" **61** AO.
"Holy Spirit" **61** N.

   Its held that Yom Kippur is the Highest Holy Day in Judaism. It is referenced to as "The Day of Atonement" and carries a ripple throughout the year. The Rabbis teach that on Yom Kippur our "fate is sealed" for the entire following year. However that fate isn't decided until the end of the day, so you have time to 'say your prayers'. For this reason only the High Cohen of Israel is allowed inside the Temple Chambers to pray on that day. This is a high holiday about atonement for sins, just as the "Holy Bible" is a book about atonement for sins.

"The Day Of Atonement" **74** N.
"Fate Is Sealed" **74** RN.
"Holiday" **74** AO.

"Yom Kippur" *45* RN.
"Holy Bible" *45* N. *45* RN.

On "Yom Kippur", October 4th, 2022 Arron Judge broke the American League record for home runs in a single season. He passed the previous record of *61* home runs, that record being set in 19*61*, coincidentally *61* years before Judge would break it. Again we see the number *61* coinciding with Jewish themes. Again, *61* is the *18th* Prime and Baseball is a game of *18* half innings and *108* double stitches on the baseball. *~ How Many Stitches Are On A Baseball? Fanbuzz.com.* Arron Judge wears jersey #99. In light of all this know that the holiday is commonly referred to as "Judgment" Day. *~ Judgment Day: Four asteroids to fly past Earth on Yom Kippur – NASA. Jerusalempost.com.*

"Baseball" *18* N.

"Judgement" 99 AO.
"Yom Kippur" 99 RAO.
Arron Judge wears jersey #99.

The Babylonian myths of the great flood state; "On the seventh day of their resting on Mount Nisir he sent out a dove, which finding no place to land, returned and then he sent out a raven which did not return so he knew it was safe. When he went out of his boat he made a sacrifice to the gods.".
Rather inverted from the account in,
Genesis 8:6-9 ESV
"**6** At the end of forty days Noah opened the window of the ark that he had made **7** and sent forth a raven. It went to and fro until the waters were dried up from the earth. **8** Then he sent forth a dove from him, to see if the waters had subsided from the face of the ground.**9** But the dove found no place to set her foot, and she returned to him to the ark, for the waters were still on the face of the whole earth. So he put out his hand and took her and brought her into the ark with him."

In the Talmud, doves are compared to the spirit of the Divine hovering over water, just like a female dove hovers over her young, tending to them in a gentle and compassionate manner. In the Hebrew Bible, doves or young pigeons are acceptable burnt offerings for those who cannot afford a more expensive animal. It is thus understood that the dove can be seen as a symbol of "Mercy".

יונה   **71** HG (Dove)
"Mercy" **71** RAO.
"The Spirit Of God" **171** AO.
Genesis 1:2 ESV
The earth was without form and void, and darkness was over the face of the deep. And **the Spirit of God** was *hovering* over the face of the waters.

In Islam, doves are well respected because they are believed to have assisted the prophet of Islam, Muhammad, at the cave of Thaw'r. Muhammad and Abu Bakr Al-Siddiq were running from Quraysh warriors, who came across the cave, deciding to hide. Two doves built a nest and laid eggs while spiders wove webs at the entrance, serving as a distraction to Muhammad's enemies, who believed the prophet could not be hiding in the cave, as the nest and webs were not disturbed.

After Jesus was baptized there was a "dove" seen over in the sky (Mathew 3:16). While modern christians will use this as a 'miraculous proof' of Jesus, the symbol of the dove is actually a quite common mythical symbol. Ancient Greeks regarded doves as symbols of immortality, rebirth, and love. Doves brought ambrosia, which represented longevity, to Mount Olympus, where the gods and goddess would drink or eat it. Greek goddess Aphrodite was also often depicted with doves surrounding her. These docile birds are known to be a symbol for navigation, for their ability to deliver messages, a practice that has been traced back to 3000 BC in Ancient Egypt. It's not until the dove flys over Jesus, that the 'Holy Spirit' enters him and he becomes 'Christ'.

"The Dove At Jesus Baptism" *74* N.
"God's Holy Spirit" *74* RN.
"Jesus Christ" *74* RN.
"Jesus" *74* AO.
"Messiah" *74* AO.

Building on this messianic symbolism there is the Hebrew interpretation that 'the messiah' or "The Anointed One", will bring in world peace and reign as a leader during the time of adjusting to world peace. The Greeks, with their pantheon of demi-gods and heroes saw in the Old Testament a different archetype. With their Hellenized world view they saw this messiah as one who had to suffer greatly in order to lessen the sufferings of others. So then, to anoint this hero and make him equal to 'God' in the stories of the gospels, the Greek authors use a "περιστερά" (Dove). As shown the symbol gives illusion to "The Holy Spirit", which Jesus now takes into himself becoming Christ.

Mathew 3:16 ESV
"And when Jesus was baptized, immediately he went up from the water, and behold, the heavens were opened to him, and he saw **the Spirit of God** descending like a dove and coming to rest on him."

"All Is Number" **171** RAO.
"The Spirit Of God" **171** AO
יונה   **71** HG. (Dove)
"Mercy" **71** RAO.

"The Anointed One" *67* RN.
"Blood Sacrifice" *67* N.
"Human Sacrifice" *67* N.
"The Dove At The Baptism of Jesus Christ" 331 AO.
331 is the *67th* Prime Number in sequence of Primes.

"The Holy Spirit" *167* AO.
John 16:7 ESV
"Nevertheless, I tell you the truth: it is to your advantage that I go away, for if I do not go away, the Helper will not come to you. But if I go, I will send him to you."

The Greek word for 'dove' would be "περιστερά". Important to note is that, at this point Jesus receives the Christ and becomes one with God seen by witnesses as a dove passing overhead. This concept is reemphasized in Revelation 1:8 "'I am the Alpha and the Omega,' says the Lord God, 'who is and who was and who is to come, the Almighty.'". The Greek letter (A) Alpha has a value of 1 and the Greek letter (Ω) Omega a value of 800.

"περιστερά" 801 GI (Dove)
"ΑΩ" 801 (Alpha and Omega)

"I am the Alpha and the Omega" 187 AO.
"All God's Prophets" 187 AO.
187 Chapters in Torah

If you take every character in the Greek Isopsephy alphabet system and add them up you will get the value 4005. Consider the fact that the majority of authoritative original manuscripts that comprise the 'New Testament' of "The Holy Bible" were written down in Greek.

"Α Β Γ Δ Ε Ζ Η Θ F I K Λ M N Ξ O Π P Σ T Y Φ X Ψ Ω"   4005 GI
"Holy Bible" 45 N. 45 RN

The English words 'Holy Spirit' would be rendered as "Ἅγιον Πνεῦμα" in Greek. If we take those words an apply Greek Isopsephy we find that it sums to 709. This is interesting because 709 is the **127th** Prime in sequence of Primes. Remember the opening words of the chapter coming from the Greek philosopher? "All is Number".

"Ἅγιον Πνεῦμα" 709 GI. (Holy Spirit)
"God's Holy Spirit" 79 N.
709 is the **127**[th] Prime Number in sequence of Primes.

"All is Number" **127** AO. 171 RAO. *72* RN.
"The Spirit Of God" 171 AO. *72* RN.

The English word "immortality" is rendered as "Ανηθικότητα" in Greek. It is insightful to notice how the "power" of immortality is bestowed to Jesus only after he is already dead. The number seven also denotes completion at the Crucifixion, Jesus spoke **seven** statements while suffering the cross:
1."Father, forgive them" Luke 23:34. **2.**"Truly, I say to you, today you will be with me in Paradise" Luke 23:43. **3.**"Woman, behold, your son!" John 19:26-27. **4.** "My God, my God, why have you forsaken me?" Matthew 27:46. **5.**"I thirst," John 19:28. **6.** "It is finished" John 19:30. **7.** "Father, into your hands I commit my spirit!" Luke 23:46.
In the context of perfection and eternal life, Jesus spoke giving **seven** parables: **1.** The bread of life John 6:35; **2.** The light of the world John 8:12; **3.** The gate to salvation John 10:9; **4.** The good shepherd John 10:11; **5.** The resurrection and the life

John 11:25-26; **6**. The way, the truth, and the life John 14:6; and **7**. The vine John 15:5. When Jesus was asked how we should pray Mathew 6:9-13, in response, Jesus gave the Lord's Prayer. Notably, the Lord's Prayer contains **seven** petitions.

"Power" **77** AO.
"Christ" **77** AO.
"Ανηθικότητα" **777** GI (Immortality)
"Immortality" **70** RN.

The concept of harmony was so critical to realizing in the Greek schools because; if it is realized that the external world, 'nature', in all respects the macro is held in a sort of harmonious law, towards perfection, towards improvement with ever refined expressions, then what implications would that hold on micro respect in regards to the individual soul? The state of achieving such an enlightenment was described as "Ἁρμονία ψυχή" in English it would be said 'A harmony of the soul". Johannes Kepler titled his masterpiece "Harmonices Mundi". In Keplers book is detailed musical harmony as being a product of man, derived from angles, in contrast to a harmony that he refers to as being 'a phenomenon that interacts with the human soul'. In turn, this allowed Kepler to claim the "Earth" has a soul because it is subjected to an astrological harmony.

"Harmonices mundi" 239 RAO. (239 is the *52nd* Prime in sequence of Primes.)
"Earth" *52* AO.

Think of how the ancients believed in the 7 classical planets as expressed in the introduction, Earth would be the 8th. Thus the Universe in Harmony with the man on earth would be the **8** and **1**. Influenced by 'mother nature' and 'father time' mankind seeks improvement throughout ages and environments.

"A Harmony Of The Soul" **81** N. **81** RN.
"Honest" **81** AO. **81** RAO.
"Evolve" **81** AO. **81** RAO.
"The Son" **81** AO **81** RAO.

Revelation 14:4 ESV
"These have been redeemed from mankind as first fruits for God and the Lamb,"
קדם   144 HG (to precede, to come before)
"The Universe In Harmony With Man"
144 N. 144 RN.

SQUARING THE CIRCLE- A geometric problem discussed among the Greeks was the challenge of constructing a square with the area of a circle by using only a finite number of steps with a compass and straightedge. Pappus in his work Mathematical

Collection states; *"There are, we say, three types of problem in geometry, the so-called 'plane', 'solid', and 'linear' problems. Those that can be solved with straight line and circle are properly called 'plane' problems, for the lines by which such problems are solved have their origin in a plane. Those problems that are solved by the use of one or more sections of the cone are called 'solid' problems. For it is necessary in the construction to use surfaces of solid figures, that is to say, cones. There remain the third type, the so-called 'linear' problem. For the construction in these cases curves other than those already mentioned are required, curves having a more varied and forced origin and arising from more irregular surfaces and from complex motions."*

If you observe the Greek title given to Jesus, "κύριος Ιησούς Χριστός", translated to English it would read as 'Lord Jesus Christ', we see that it equates to **3168** in GI. In the Septuagint, κύριος is regularly used to translate יהוה. Notice the four letter name while we are talking about four sided Squares.

"κύριος Ιησούς Χριστός" =   **3168** GI
3+1+6+8=*18* The Hebrew number of life

.

Now this is interesting because its been calculated by modern mathematicians that the Mean diameter of Earth = 7920 miles. The average Diameter taken through the center of Earth from the Tropic of

Cancer to the Tropic of Capricorn = 7920 miles.
Keeping with the concept of 'squaring the circle',
envision the earth with a line representing the
diameter in view, taking that same size line, lay four
of those outstretched equator lines perfectly around
the sphere of the earth.

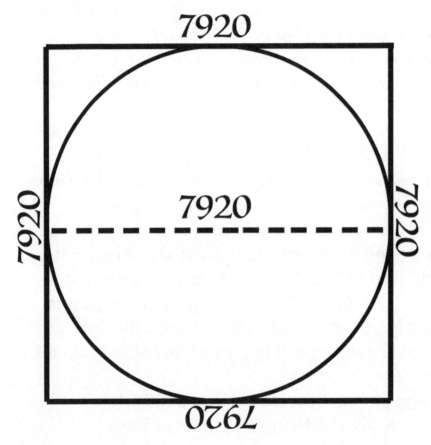

7920 x 4= **31,680**
7920+7920+7920+7920= **31,680**
"κύριος Ιησούς Χριστός" **3168** GI
(Lord Jesus Christ)

PYTHAGOREAN THEORM – Of the many lessons from the Greek's still with us, is the Pythagorean Theorem. Expressed as a^2 +b^2 = c^2, often used to find the length of an unknown side of a right triangle. In the hands of tradesmen and builders, the Pythagorean Theorem becomes the 3-4-5 proportion method for establishing square layout lines or checking a project to make sure its angles are square. The 3-4-5 method works as follows:

On one side of a corner, measure 3 inches (or some multiple of 3 inches) from the corner and make a mark. On the opposite side of the corner, measure 4 inches (or the same multiple of 4 inches) from the corner and make a mark. Next, measure between the two marks. If the distance is 5 inches (or the appropriate multiple of 5), your corner is square. The key element here is the ratio used, not the unit of measurement.

A statue depicting Pythagoras can be found on Samos Island. ~ *Samos Island Pythagorean Statue.* The triangle form that takes shape in the statue is an obvious tribute to the Pythagorean Theorem. The statue resembles a modern symbol seen across the U.S. on many church campuses. That symbol being the cross on its side or the carried cross. In Christian philosophy the symbol conveys how Jesus, literally carried out the sacrificial will of God. The carried cross makes a right triangle with the ground or mount it sits atop being the bottom line.

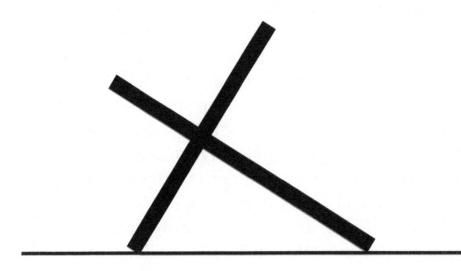

This is profound if you consider with these key factors of 3,4, and 5. We see the holy name אֵל שַׁדַּי translating in English as 'God Almighty' equals 345 in HG. When Moses asked God his name in Exodus 3:13, God responds saying, אהיה אשר אהיה translating 'I will be what I will be'. This sums to 543 in HG, the same numbers reversed.

Exodus 3:14

ויאמר אלהים אל־משה אֶהְיֶה אֲשֶׁר אֶהְיֶה ויאמר כה תאמר לבני ישראל אהיה שלחני אליכם

Exodus 3:14 ESV

God said to Moses, "I AM WHO I AM." And he said, "Say this to the people of Israel: 'I AM has sent me to you.'"

If we then add 345 + 543 = **888**. The number **8** that makes the infinity sign when rotated ∞.

אֵל שַׁדַּי   <u>345</u> HG (God Almighty)

אהיה אשר אהיה   <u>543</u> HG (I Will Be What I Will Be)

"ιησούς"   **888** GI (Jesus)

<u>345</u>+<u>543</u>=**888**

God Almighty + I Will Be What I Will Be = Jesus?

    In light of this information you may be astounded at what is to be found if you add up the verse totals of the 4 passages describing the dove or Holy Spirit from the 4 Gospel authors. Mathew *3:16*, Mark *1:10*, Luke *3:22*, John *1:32*.

316 + 110 + 322 + 132 = **880**

"Gospel" **88** RAO.

"Occult" **88** RAO.

<u>"For Flesh And Blood Has Not Revealed This To You"</u> **457** AO. (Pg. 33).

457 is the **88**[th] Prime Number in sequence of Primes

"ιησούς"   **888** GI (Jesus)

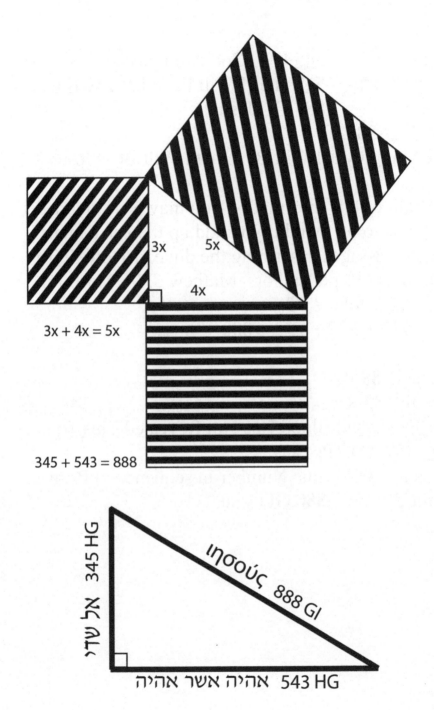

3x

5x

4x

3x + 4x = 5x

345 + 543 = 888

345 HG אל שלי

וחסוע 888 GI

543 HG אהיה אשר אהיה

Notice how the Greek alphabet can be separated into three equal groups of **8** based on numerical value; **8**-monads; **8**-decads; **8**-hundreds. Fittingly, this system is known as the "Greek Ionic System", dating back to the **8th** Century BCE. The number **8** that makes the infinity sign when rotated ∞. Just as Gods son, "Jesus", which in Greek translates as "ιησούς", has a value of **888** in GI.

"Greek Ionic System" **80** N.
"ἀνάλημμα"   170 GI (Analemma ∞) 1+7+0= **8**
Α Β Γ Δ Ε Ζ Η Θ **(8 Single Digits (1s)**
Ι Κ Λ Μ Ν Ξ Ο Π **(8 Double Digits (10s)**
Ρ Σ Τ Υ Φ Χ Ψ Ω **(8 Triple Digits (100s)**

Another layer concerning the mathematical symbols of the Pythagorean Theorem is that the 3 points need a 4th. That is a realm, space to exist. The right angle triangle with its three points is a great tool to conceive of the 4th dimension and man's interaction with deity. Like the Holy Trinity, 3, is used to 'point' to 1 God which creates a 4th in totality (3 . 1 4). The parable sits even older as the 4 letter name of God in Hebrew "YHVH" is 4 letters long but actually uses 3 letters total. (Y. H^2. V.)

PI-There are patterns that naturally occur in the Universe, patterns we've discovered in life. The Golden Ratio is one of them. Even animals, plants, and insects have manifestations of this geometric pattern. Interestingly not just in nature but also the ancient establishments have this symmetry.

When thinking of important numbers one may think of the perfect number, **3.14** or π. It can be calculated approximately by 22/7. Know that there are 27 Letters in the Greek Isopsephy system, corresponding to the 27 books in the Greek New Testament. The Pi formula is used to represent the perfect patterns of manifestations across forms in nature. One should be aware that in the Sepher Yetzirah the act of God creating the universe is described as "חקק וחצב". Translating this to English would be, 'inscribed and carved'. Is the manifestation of pi in nature hinting to the presence of unseen forces or simply coincidence? Are these mathematic formulas keys to understanding the universe? Are these interpretations attempting to describe reality or is this reality itself expressed in numbers?

שַׁדָּי   **314** HG (Almighty)
חקק וחצב   **314** HG (Inscribed and Carved)
"Mathematics is the alphabet with which God has written the Universe" **314** RN.
"The English Alphabet" **314** RAO.
"Holy Blood of Jesus Christ" **314** RAO.
"The Blood of Jesus Christ" **314** RAO.
"Twenty Two Divided By Seven" **314** AO.
22/7= **3.14285714**

"Three Hundred Sixty" <u>227</u> AO.
360° in a perfect circle.

   We read in Luke that he gives <u>3</u> sets of <u>14</u>
generations from Abraham to Jesus, a reference to π?
<u>3.14</u>. The only reason the ancestral line is given is
because, according to biblical prophecy the messiah
has to be from the line of דוד, David. Realizing that
<u>3×14</u> = **42**, let us read now Verse **4:2** from the
concluding book of the Old Testament or what the
Greeks would have called the "Septuagint", Malachi.
Luke 1:17 ESV "So all the generations from
Abraham to David were fourteen generations, and
from David to the deportation to Babylon fourteen
generations, and from the deportation to Babylon to
the Christ fourteen generations."
Malachi **4:2** ESV "But for you who fear my name,
<u>the sun</u> of righteousness shall rise with healing in its
wings. You shall go out leaping like calves from the
stall."

דוד   **14** HG (David)

<u>3×14</u> = **42**
"Septuagint" **42** N.
"Savior" **42** RAO.
"Sin" **42** AO.

PERFECT NUMBERS- Pythagoras was fascinated by the concept of "Perfect Numbers". He had expressed belief that 4 represented God, at that time in history only 4 Perfect Numbers were known to exist. Those were numbers 6, **28**, 496 and 8,128. To date, Perfect Numbers are still being discovered, with the latest discovery coming in 2016, and it was the 49th number in sequence of Perfect Numbers found. Not arbitrary to this point is that the 4th book of the Bible is titled, "Numbers".

Perfect Numbers EX: 1, 2, 3 and 6 divide into 6. When you calculate for a Perfect Number, you add all the divisors, except for the one that is the number itself. So in the case of 6, that means you add 1+2+3 = 6.

What is interesting about the number **28** and how it connects to "Man'? God created man on the 6th day of creation. Ponder how many beats a heart makes in a day, how the body can self repair from injuries, how as a species we chose to adapt and overcome our imperfections, pressing on toward perfection. Why waste time entertaining the ideas of perfection and numbers? To the Kabbalist, numbers are seen as a means to interpret God, because God is seen as the calculated Master Mathematician. Man was created on the 6th day, the 6th commandment is 'Not to Murder' another man. 6 is the 1st Perfect Number, and **28** is the 2nd Perfect Number.

"Number" **28** N.
"Man" **28** AO.
"Colors" **28** N.

"Perfect Numbers" 213 RAO. 2+1=3
"Thou Art The Christ" 213. 2+1=3
"Peace On Earth 213 RAO. 2+1=3
"Book Of Isaiah" 213 RAO. 2+1=3
Isaiah 11:9 ESV
"They shall not hurt or destroy in all my holy
mountain; for the earth shall be full of the knowledge
of the Lord as the waters cover the sea."

   You have invested into yourself a solid foundation
on which to see and interpret the Biblical & Spiritual
significance of number values in the modern day.
Without having spiritual insights the true symbolic
gesture of modern day rituals would be lost upon
many. I do apologize for not covering the bible in it's
entirety. If there were verses not covered that you
feel were more important than what was presented I
encourage you to apply what has been taught,
making discoveries for yourself is undoubtedly the
best way to practice your new found tool of
Gematria. As it has been proven, the names and
concepts involved in the verses have been named in
English to convey a Gematria significance. Now we
will apply this biblical study to modern society.

GOVERNMENT & POLITICS

"I'm from the government, and I'm here to help."
-Ronald Reagan

Seeing that 74 is an important and reoccurring number around God, lets see how those who play god venerate the inverse. How else would they be able to play god unless they were the "Authority"? What is authority in the modern sense if not the "Government"? Here in America, the puppet ruler of our nation is referred to as the "President". The president resides in "D.C." and keeping true to Catholic symbolism our president gets to stay in the pure "White House". Constant pundits can be heard spouting on about how the "foundation" of America will shift every 4 or 8 years. Funny enough the president is elected in November but not inaugurated until January. Meaning that if a president only serves one term his replacement wins the office **47** months later. In our time who are the ones that declare the president and the daily on goings, would it be the "News"? If someone is to go against the authority and their unjust laws you might find yourself in front of a "judge" wearing all black, eager to bang their "gavel". In our government system there are only two parties of significance, the "Democrats" and "Republicans". The Republicans descend from the "Whig" party. Their most famous member of the party being President Lincoln, who gave his famous

Gettysburg address which starts, "**4** score and **7** years ago".

Not contrary recent president, Barack Obama was 'elected' into office at age **47**. "Trump" was the president, famous for his "Twitter" rants. However "TIME" Magazine put out their person of the year, which was actually two people. Sleepy Joe Biden, and the person who would become the **47**[th] president should Biden take an early exit, Kamala Harris. Which reminds one of Trump yelling out during the debate "I've done more in **47** months as president than you did in **47** years Joe!". The actor Trump being famous for his show "The Apprentice" mockery at its finest.

The masonic compass symbol which originated in "France" is set at **47°**. Realize the nations birthday the 4th of July can also be expressed **4/7**. Further masonic symbolism can be found in the **47**[th] problem of Euclid on which there is much detailed literature, but briefly condensed is a mathematical and allegorical concept on how to establish the perfect "foundation" (pg. 135). The foundation for Washington, D.C. was laid on 9-18-1793, $9+18+1+7+9+3=$**47**. Interestingly enough the New International Translation of the bible uses the word "Satan" **47** times. This is interesting because of the demonization of old religions which primarily revolved around the sun. Remember the sun travels between the tropics of Capricorn and Cancer to the tune of **47°** every year.

"Authority" **47** N.
"Government" **47** RN.
"White House" **47** RN.
"D.C." **47** RAO.
"Vatican" **47** RN.
"Foundation" **47** N.
"Judge" **47** AO.
"Gavel" **47** AO.
"Democrat" **47** RN.
"Republican" **47** N.
"Whig" **47** AO.
"Trump" **47** RAO.
"The Apprentice" **211** RAO (211 is the **47**[th] Prime Number in sequence of Primes.)
"Twitter" **47** RN.
"Police Man" **47** RN.
"TIME" **47** AO.
"France" **47** AO.
"Francis" **47** RN.
"News" **47** RAO.
"Vibration" **47** N.

In light of the topic of Masonry lets look at a number stooped in occult lure. 33 the number of pairs of vertebra in the human spinal column which the stem of the brain sits atop. This is important to note for those interested in the correspondence with numbers and man's body. Also there is an entire spiritual school, which allegories revolve around spiritual ascension up the vertebra into the "pineal" gland. Keep in mind many contend Jesus died at age 33. What is Masonry in the modern day but a group willing to keep "secrecy". There are higher degrees in masonry, a noteworthy being the 33rd degree. The level of Confederate general Albert Pike who had a statue in Washington D.C. until June 2020. In Albert Pike's magnum opus, Morals and Dogma, he remarks on Kabbalah, "all the Masonic associations owe to it their Secrets and their Symbols.". In Washington D.C. right in the heart of our "federal" capitol is the headquarters of the "order" of the Scottish Rite, known as The House of the Temple, which has an exterior of 33 pillars each 33 feet tall. On the fraternal 'order' of police's logo there is depicted a handshake, something typically associated with masonry. ~ *'Each column is a monolith, meaning it was carved from a single piece of stone! The Temple's stately Ionic colonnade is comprised of 33 columns, each 33 feet high, honoring the 33 degrees of the Scottish Rite.' Each column comprising the*

House of the Temple's colonnade was built in three sections. Scottishrite.org.

"Pineal" *30* N. <u>33</u> RN.
"Secrecy" <u>33</u> N
"Federal" <u>33</u> N.
"Gnostic" <u>33</u> N.
"Order" *60* AO. <u>33</u> N. *30* RN
"Police" *60* AO. <u>33</u> N. *30* RN.

George W. Bush graduated from Yale in 1968, the same year 9-1-1 was made the national emergency dialing code, the same year WTC construction began, also the same year the movie '2001: Space Odyssey' came out. The joke of course being that in 2001 Space Odyssey their spaceship is overtaken by an A.I.. Bush became president in the midst of controversy. For months before the election date many pundits reported on how important the state of Florida would be. Coincidentally enough Jeb Bush was the 43rd governor of Florida at the time. Regardless of the demand for recount George W. Bush became the 43rd President. Improving on his father George H. W. Bush's legacy as the 43rd Vice President.

"Yale" 43 AO.
"Florida" 43 RN.
"Masonic" 43 RN

It has become public knowledge that Bush was a member of the 'Skull and Bones' fraternity at "Yale". When Bush and Kerry were interviewed by Tim Russert he asked both candidates directly "You're both in Skull and Bones, what does that mean for America?", "The numbers 322, 223 what does it mean?". To which both candidates replied "It's a secret". The only man to pass away since the interview occurred is Tim Russert. He died June 13th, 2008 including that day in the count, it was 38 days after his May 7th, 2008 birthday. ~ *Bush and Kerry discuss Skull and Bones- Meet The Press. Youtube.com.*

"Skull and Crossbones" 223 AO.
"Population Control" 223 RAO.
"Desecration Of Human Life" 223 AO.

"Murder" 38 RN.
"Death" 38 AO.
"Gematria" 38 N.

Barack Obama ran for president with the campaign slogan "Hope". He made history becoming the first African American to hold the presidential office. No doubt a major moment in Civil Rights history. Interestingly enough Obama became president 44 years after the Civil Rights act of 1964. I also found it curious how "Barack Hussein Obama" became

president just 4 years after the death of Saddam
Hussein.

"Hope" 44 AO. 64 RAO. (Obama the 44th president)
"Barack Hussein Obama" 64 N.
Becomes President 44 years after 1964 civil rights
act.

   There was much controversy raised when a
popular biblical tv show 'The Bible' depicted the
Satan character with an actor that strongly resembled
Barack Obama.~ *'The Bible': Satan Actor Looks Like
Obama In History Channel Miniseries.
Huffpost.com.* It is interesting to note that the bible
states that Satan fell like a lightning bolt from
heaven.
Luke 10:18 ESV
And he said to them, "I saw Satan fall like lightning
from heaven."
Notice that the Hebrew word, בָּרָק, which would be
pronounced 'Ba Ra Q', translates as, 'Lightning'. On
August 4th, 2022 the white house was reportedly
struck by lightning, causing the death of 3 people
and leaving 1 injured. August 4th is Barack Hussein
Obama's birthday.~ *Lightning strike near white
house leaves 3 dead 1 injured. Nypost.com.*

   Martin Luther King Jr. took the name latter in life,
after the Reverend Martin Luther. Martin Luther was

famous for writing the 95 Thesis against the Catholic church. On April 4th, 1967 MLK gave a speech entitled 'Beyond Vietnam A Time To Break Silence'. This date can be written **4-4**. In the speech he encouraged all to look at the military industrial complex. Pointing out the tactics of dehumanization used to brain wash young men into killing people because they are different. Exactly a year later, April 4th, 1968 MLK was assassinated in a 'shooting'. Now because 1968 was a leap year that means that April 4th was the 95th day of the year. The number 4 is associated with death being that in Japanese the word for 'death' and the word for '4' are pronounced the same way. 4 is spelled 四 and Death is spelled 死, the English transliteration for both is 'Shi'.

"Military" **44** N.
"Officer" **44** N.
"Trooper" **44** N.
"Kill" **44** AO.
"Shooting" **44** N.

"Martin" *42* RN.
In the sitcom 'Martin' staring Martin Lawrence, the family lives in apartment # *42*

Donald Trump had his Mar-A-Lago mansion raided by the FBI on the date August 8th, 2022. That is a date that is written **8-8**. Rather interesting in retrospect because in his first campaign as president he had the message "Text TRUMP to __88022__". Who could forget the coverage about "Trump" being endorsed by **88** military generals during his campaign?~ *Why Donald Trump's Endorsement by 88 Generals Is So Dangerous ~ yahoonews.com.* Business Insider wrote an article with a headline so stupendous it should've clued all into number symbolism.~ *People are concerned that an $**88** baseball sold on the Trump Organization's merch page could be a secret message to white supremacists. Businessinsider.com.* On July 16th, 2018 Fox News felt it was necessary to report that Trump had raised $**88** million for his re-election campaign.~ *Trump raises more than $**88M** in re-election campaign: report. Foxnews.com.* On October 5th, 2017 multiple news outlets reported "'Maybe it's the calm before the storm' Pres. Trump says alongside US military leaders. 'You'll find out.'". From the date that news broke, 10-5-2017 counting to the date that the Coronavirus pandemic was declared, 3-11-2020, is a total of **888** days.~ *President Trump Warns of 'the Calm Before the Storm' During Military Meeting. Timemagazine.com*

"Trump" **88** AO.

On Feburary 20th, 2020 before the killing of George Floyd, there were many news outlets covering Trump. Trump was saying that Minnesota senator Amy Klobuchar 'choked' during the 2020 democratic party debates. Many articles made sure to put 'choked' in quotes. While Trump was knocking her, he had went as far to say "She couldn't breathe.". ~ *Trump: Bloomberg, Klobuchar 'choked' in Democratic debate. Thehill.com.* Amy Klobuchar's birthday is May 25th, the same day that George Floyd was killed. May 25th is in the zodiacal period of Gemini, known as 'The Twins'. Minnesota is known for the twin cities, Amy Klobuchar and George Floyd are Minnesota natives. Notice the Gematria value of **46** in the word 'choked', and that George Floyd, age **46**, was choked to death.

"Choked" **46** AO.

On January 12th, 2021 a date written **1/12**, Donald Trump visited the "America-Mexico boarder wall". The 45th president gave a speech at the 450th mile of the new boarder wall. Correlating with Trump being 'Mr. Build A Wall' the night that he became president elect was November 9th, the same date in history as the fall of the Berlin Wall. Again Trump is the 45th president, important being that (4 + 5 = 9) and 45 is the 9th Triangular Number (1 + 2 + 3 + 4 + 5 + 6 + 7 + 8 + 9= 45). All these synchronizations with the man that became the president elect on 9/9. Aware of this information, you should watch a decade old

'Serta mattress commercial featuring Trump' stating "Looking good number 9, looking good!"

"America-Mexico Boarder Wall" **112** N.
"Mathematics" **112** AO.

After the "death" of Ruth Ginsburg, Amy Barrett was confirmed by the senate on October 26th, 2020. From the day Ginsburg died September 18th, 2020 to the date October 26th, 2020 is exactly **38** days. Ruth Ginsburg was Jewish and died on "Rosh Hashanah" which is the Jewish new year. All this revolving around the "Supreme Court".

"Death" **38** AO.
"Killing" **38** N.
"Murder" **83** RAO. **38** RN.

"Jews" <u>57</u> AO.
"Rosh Hashanah" <u>57</u> N.
"Supreme Court" <u>57</u> N.

The biggest number in the 2020 presidential election was undoubtedly **46**, which is unsurprising considering that Joe Biden is the **46th** president. Biden who's son Beau Biden died at age **46**. Not to mention that his first wife and daughter died in 1972, 47 years before he became "president" elect. Which relates to the fact that he was the 47th person to hold the title of Vice President. However Biden didn't officially enter the Senate until 19*73*, **46** years before becoming president. Don't forget that Biden is a proud Catholic, which is the religion that has **46** books in their Old Testament and *73* books in total. The only other Catholic president was JFK, the *35ᵗʰ* president, who died at age **46**. Another death synced with the election was the death of Supreme Court Justice, Ruth Bader Ginsberg, who died on September 18ᵗʰ, 2020. September 18ᵗʰ, 2020 was exactly **46** days before the November 3ʳᵈ, 2020 presidential election. The date of the election November 3ʳᵈ, 2020 took place exactly **46** weeks, or 322 days, after the pope's December 17ᵗʰ, 2019 birthday. After the election results were announced by the media declaring Biden the winner, which they have no right to declare, Trump didn't concede defeat until November 15ᵗʰ, 2020. Although he did make these remarks sarcastically claiming "Biden won the rigged election". However isn't it telling that Trump waited until the day leaving **46** days left in the year to make these remarks? From the day his wife died November 20ᵗʰ, 1972 to the day he was elected "senator" on December 18ᵗʰ, 1972 is exactly 29 days.

"Senator" 29 N.
"Sacrifice" *73* AO. **46** N.
Genesis 46 begins with a sacrifice
"Ritual Sacrifice" *73* N.

"Catholic" **46** RN.
"Joe Biden" **64** AO. 44 RN.
64 the reflection of **46**, and notice the 44 in light of him running along side Obama, the 44th president.
"Dean Koontz" **46** RN.
Author of the 'novel' from 1981 about a virus out of China, which is taking place during the **46**th presidential election.

   Although American citizens were pressed to find grass roots supporters of "President Biden" during the election, it was nevertheless reported that Biden received the most votes for a presidential candidate ever! The total amount of votes reported being 81 million.~ *DNC Reminds Trump: 81 Million Americans Voted for Biden. Democrats.org.* While its easy to believe there were millions that didn't want to vote for Trump, reflect for a moment. Biden is reported to have received more support than Obama, or any other candidate in history for that matter. Are these reportings what logical observation would imply or rather what ritualistic Gematria implication implies? ~ *Joe Biden breaks Obama's record for 'most votes ever cast for a U.S. presidential candidate'. cbsnews.com*

"President Biden" 81 RN.
"Votes" 81 AO.

"Most Votes Ever Cast For A U.S. Presidential Candidate" 181 N.

On May 4th, 2021 Joe Biden stated that he wanted **70%** of America taking the vaccination for "corona virus" by "Independence Day". Later in the year on August 2nd, 2021 the Associated Press reported that **70%** of Americans had taken the "covid vaccine". August 2nd is the 214th day of the year.

"Corona Virus" **70** RN.
"Independence Day" **70** RN.
"Covid Vaccine" 214 RAO. **70** RN.

Another number that frequently presented itself was **71**. In an article presented by MSN, they stated that the Five Thirty Eight model gave Biden a **71%** chance of winning the election. On super Tuesday Biden was declared to receive **71%** of the African American vote. His vice president being "Kamala Devi Harris" a woman of color relating to the fact that Joe was the running mate of the only president of color. Not unrelated was the headlines about the movie "Birth of a Nation", a movie following the life of Nat Turner. The movie claimed it had opened with the box office release grossing $**7.1** million. Nat Turner died on November 11th 1831. (11+11+18+31=**71**) If you're aware of this you may have noticed how the first Democratic Debate of

2020 opened with a question posed to Elizabeth Warren about how "**71**% of Americans say the economy is doing well".

"Kamala Devi Harris" **71** N.
"African American" **71** N.
"Catholic" **71** AO.

    Something related to the planet Venus is the symbol of the pearl. This is depicted in, The Birth of Venus a painting by the Italian artist Sandro Botticelli, probably made in the mid 1480s. The goddess Venus is arriving at the shore after her birth, when she had emerged from the sea fully-grown. Notice the shell she is standing on, as pearls emerge from oyster shells. In regards to this I couldn't help notice the headline by 'Who What Wear' that claims 'Kamala Harris Has Been Wearing Her Signature Accessory for **35** Years'.

"Mother of Pearls" <u>207</u> RAO.
"Venus" <u>27</u> RN.
"Female VP" **35** N.
"Catholic" **35** N.

    To further establish the connections of the past lets look deeper into the things reported to us about the modern Pope. "Jorge Mario Bergoglio" is the first publicly Jesuit pope. He prefers to stay in suite **201** of the "Domus Sanctae Marthae"~ *Inside Casa Santa Marta, Pope Francis's New Digs. NationalGeographic.com.* "The Jesuit Order" at one point in history were outlawed by the Catholic Church only being saved by Catherine the Great, who reportedly saved exactly **201** Jesuit Knights. ~ *How the Jesuits Survived Their Suppression. Saint Joseph's University Press.com.* The man who founded the Jesuit order was known as "Ignatius of Loyola" a name summing to **201**.

All these **201s** could remind one of the Event **201** Simulation, which took place October 18th 2019. The theory being there is an average of two hundred outbreaks a year and what would happen if there was one more. If one simulation isn't enough for you look into the 'Clade X' simulation which took place May 15th, 2018. From May 15th, 2018 to the date the Coronavirus was declared a pandemic March 11th, 2020 is exactly 666 days. *https://www.centerforhealthsecurity.org/our-work/exercises/event201/..*

"Jorge Mario Bergoglio" *112* N.
"Catholicism" *112* AO.

"Ignatius of Loyola" **201** AO.
"The Jesuit Order" **201** RAO.
"Domus Sanctae Marthae" **201** AO.
"Stay the Fuck at Home" **201** AO. (Next paragraph)

"George Perry Floyd" **201** AO.
"Wuhan Four Hundred" **201** AO.

"Event two o one" <u>56</u> N.
"Coronavirus" *155* AO. <u>56</u> N
May 15th, *15/5* date of Clade X simulation
"Twenty-Twenty" <u>56</u> RN.
"Society of Jesus" <u>56</u> N.

    The term "Coronavirus" has been engraved into our minds by the man "Anthony Fauci" who graduated from the Cornell Medical College, Cornell University being a Jesuit college. I encourage you to watch his speech at George Town University, also a Jesuit University, on January 11th, 2017. ~ *"During a forum on pandemic preparedness at Georgetown University, Fauci said the Trump administration will not only be challenged by ongoing global health threats such as influenza and HIV, but also a surprise disease outbreak. "The history of the last 32 years that I have been the director of the NIAID will tell the next administration that there is no doubt they will be faced with the challenges their predecessors were faced with," he said.".* **<u>Fauci: 'No doubt' Trump will face surprise infectious disease outbreak</u>**. *Healionews.com*. Again this article released January 11th, 2017 more than 3 years before the pandemic declaration.

Following the outbreak the media exercised their "mind control" abilities by scaring the public into buying excess amounts of "toilet paper". Also remember at the start of the pandemic when the California governor "Gavin Newsom" predicted that **56%** of California's population – roughly 25.5 million residents – could be infected with the 'novel' Coronavirus over an eight-week period. A week being seven days long the prediction being that it would take eight weeks for **56%**, $7\times8=$ **56**. Isn't it so ripe when reporters say 'the novel virus', considering the 1981 novel by Dean Koontz? Where a virus being used as a bio-weapon originates out of China. Not unrelated is that 2020 is 'The Year of the Rat', when rats are notorious for being a cause of spreading plague. With the printing and giving away of stimulus money alongside the thousands of people that took to "unemployment" during the pandemic, the nation is suffering from its worst bout of inflation in its history. Governments have claimed that the undersupply of workers will result in "food shortage" and "fuel shortage".

"Gavin Newsom" **56** RN.
"Coronavirus" **56** N.
"Anthony Fauci" *137* AO. **56** N. *61* RN.
"Mind Control" *137* AO. **56** N. *160* RAO. *61* RN.
"Toilet Paper" *137* AO. **56** N. *160* RAO. *61* RN.
"Society of Jesus" **56** N.

"Unemployment" **56** N.
"Food Shortage" **56** RN
"Fuel Shortage" **56** N

    Holding true to the number of the year, **56**, the LSU Tigers head coach got his **56**th win at the conclusion of the 2019-2020 season. A ritual that took place with their QB, Joe Burrow who transferred from Ohio State to LSU, defeated Clemson in the finals in New Orleans and claimed the Heisman Trophy. Which is the exact story line that happened earlier in history with Billy Cannon who won the Heisman Trophy and defeated Clemson in New Orleans in 1959. Billy Cannon died on May 20th 2018. On May 20th 2018 Joe Burrow transferred to LSU. Billy Cannon wore the number 20 on his jersey this ritual taking place in 2020. Remember how the year that kicked off with the mass consumption of the idiotic 'Tiger King'. And who could forget Samuel L Jackson mocking us all, reading the book titled "Stay the Fuck at Home" on 'Jimmy Kimmel Live' with the picture of a tiger on the cover of the book.

    Following up on this ritual, Joe Burrow was drafted to the Cincinnati Bengals. He made it all the way to the super bowl in the 2021-2022 NFL Season. Along the way the Bengals first defeated the Oakland Raiders, a team that Billy Cannon played for. Next, the Bengals defeated the Tennessee

Titians, the team formerly known as the Houston Oilers, a team that Billy Cannon played for. Lastly to secure their position in the super bowl the Bengals beat the Kansas City Chiefs, a team that Billy Cannon used to play for.

During Easter 2020 the government exercised their authority over religion by telling churches they would not be allowed to gather due to the virus. The popular phrases revolving around Easter being, "He is risen" or "He has risen". Tying into Corona which is defined as the light seen around an eclipse which involves the sun. Easter wasn't established as a holiday until the Council of Nicaea where Christians adopted many festivals that revolve around the sun. Easter fell on April 12th, 2020 the *102nd* day of the year that leaves 263 days left. 263 is the **56th** Prime Number in sequence of Primes. Remember Christians were told not to meet because of "Coronavirus" which was simulated in Event *201,* the inverse of *102*, the high holy day Easter falling on the *102nd* day of the year.

"Coronavirus" **56** N. (263 days left in the year after Easter, 263 the 56th prime)
"He is Risen" **56** RN.
"He has Risen" **56** RN.
"Mind Control" **56** N.

"Propaganda" <u>177</u> RAO.
"The Easter Bunny" <u>177</u> AO. *201* RAO.
"His Resurrection" *201* AO.

"Easter Sunday" <u>44</u> N. <u>73</u> RN
"Kill" <u>44</u> AO.
"Sacrifice" <u>73</u> AO

   The Event 201 simulation took place on October 18th, 2019, a date that could be written as 10-18. Consider 10:18. March 28, 2021 saw Nike selling pairs of Lil Nas X shoes marketed to 'contain human blood'. The shoes sold out of stock in under a minute reportedly selling for $1,018 each. ~ *Lil Nas X's unofficial 'Satan' Nikes containing human blood sell out in under a minute. Cnn.com.*
Luke 10:18 ESV
And he said to them, "I saw Satan fall like lightning from heaven."

   The first government approved vaccine for Coronavirus arrived in the U.K. On December 2nd, 2020. Thanks to "Operation Warp Speed", which was funded by tax payer dollars to promote the quickest development for the "Coronavirus Vaccine". Notice the date December 2nd can be expressed <u>2-12</u> or <u>12-2.</u> which relates to the Jesuit IHS moto, which sits inside the <u>sun</u>. Remember how the U.K. Where the first vaccine was given relates to the Jesuit symbol in that it is often referenced as 'The empire on which the <u>sun</u> never sets'. This vaccine released **266** days after the declaration of a pandemic on March 3rd, 2020. The company to put out the vaccine was Pfizer. At the time of writing this, Pfizer has paid out over $2.3 BILLION in settlements. There was an article by CNN with the headline "Pfizer's CEO sold $**5.6** million in stock the day he announced promising vaccine news"

"Operation Warp Speed" **266** RAO (The vaccine was given **266** days after the pandemic declared on March 11th)
"IESUS HOMINUM SALVATOR" **266** RAO. <u>122</u> RN. (122 like the date <u>12-2</u>)
"Solar Cult" <u>122</u> RAO. (Corona a reference to the sun)
"Pope Francis" <u>122</u> AO.
"Coronavirus Vaccine" <u>212</u> AO. (212 the date 2-12)

   The pope himself released a new encyclical titled "Fratelli Tutti", in English, All Brothers, "on fraternity and social friendship". This was to cover ideals about a post "Coronavirus" world. This was released on October 3rd, 2020. October 3rd is exactly <u>75</u> days before the pope's December 17th birthday. Those who support "Trump" should look into the HUGE smile on Trumps face when he met pope Francis, leaving "Washington D.C." to visit him at the "Vatican". If you've ever seen the movie 'V for Vendetta' then you will 'Remember remember the 5th of November' which in history relates to the Jesuit plot to overthrow the British Parliament. Funny enough, November 5th is the day leaving **56** days left in the year. The attempt to overthrow Parliament is referenced as "The Gunpowder Plot"

"The Gunpowder Plot" **84** N.
"Jesuit" **84** AO.
"United States of America" **84** N.

"On Fraternity and Social Friendship" <u>351</u> AO.
"For the Greater Glory of God" <u>351</u> RAO.
<u>351</u> is the *26th* Triangular Number in sequence of Triangular Numbers. Relevant since the pope claims to be the speaker for "God", this being a "Letter" given to us by the "Papacy".

"God" *26* AO.
"Letter" *26* N.
"Papacy" *26* N.

"Pope" **56** RAO.
"Fratelli Tutti" **56** N.
"Coronavirus" **56** N.
"Mind Control" **56** N.
"Washington D.C." **56** N.

While speaking of Rome lets quickly cover some relevant Gematria terms. Washington D.C. Was consolidated in the year 1871. 1+8+7+1=<u>17</u>, like "Mason". Washington D.C. Has the nickname "Rome on the Potomac". Sometimes people will refer to it as the "**51**st" state. In light of the United States of America being considered a 'Christian Nation', why would it be so? At the current time children are taught in school that the Pilgrims came to escape the crowns and religious persecutions. Not to mention the curiosity of Pope Innocent VIII funding Christopher Columbus who, in the fairy tales, discovers North America.

"Catholic Church" *75* RN.
"Order out of Chaos" *75* N.
"Order" *75* RAO.
"New World Order" *75* N.
"Ignatius of Loyola" *75* N.

Nevertheless the nation was established July 4th, a date written <u>7-4</u>. Americas birthday is referred to as "Independence Day" and is considered a "Holiday". A strange 'coincidence' to take note of is that rivals Thomas Jefferson and Samuel Adams who were both presidents, died on the same day in history on <u>7-4-</u>**1826**. Later on, president James Monroe died on <u>7-4-</u>1831. From 7-4-**1826** to 7-4-1831 is exactly 1826 days apart, like the former two presidents died in the year **1826**. ~ *Three Presidents Die on July 4th: Just a Coincidence? Constitutioncenter.org.*

"Rome on the Potomac" <u>74</u> RN.
"Independence Day" <u>74</u> N.
"Holiday" <u>74</u> AO.
"Jesus" <u>74</u> AO.
"Fourth of Jew Lie" <u>74</u> N.
"Roman Catholicism" <u>74</u> N.

The Gregorian calendar operates off of the sun and how long it takes for the earth to travel around. The sick joke being that the "pope" implemented it after years of persecuting scientists and astrologers for proposing the same idea, which the church considered heresy. ~ *"The Church had decided the idea that the sun moved around the Earth was an absolute fact of scripture that could not be disputed, despite the fact that scientists had known for centuries that the Earth was not the center of the universe." Galileo is accused of heresy. History.com.*

Established in 1582 and <u>named after the pope</u> at the time, Gregory XIII. The Gregorian calendar replaced what was known as the Julian calendar. But not without paying tribute to Julias Cesar. With the Ides of March, set on the date March 15th, which of course is the <u>74</u>th day of the year. A story from history about the "killing" of the great Cesar, dated to the year <u>44</u> BC. The Ides of March being a day set aside to remember the "stabbing" by the senate. Not unrelated was the March 15th, 2019 New York Times headline of Cesar Sayoc pleading guilty to sending mail bombs to democratic politicians.~ *Mail Bomb Suspect Accused of Targeting Clinton, Obama and Other Democrats to Plead Guilty. Nytimes.com.*

"Pope" <u>52</u>
<u>52</u> weeks in the year, Calendar named after a pope

"Stabbing" <u>74</u> AO. <u>52</u> RN.
 "Killing" <u>74</u> AO.
"Roman Catholicism" <u>74</u> N.

More compounding evidence came through the CDC headlines. ~ *CDC and Health Partners Responding to Monkeypox Case in the U.S.. cdc.gov.* The CDC put out an 'Immediate Release' on May 18th, 2022. Which is the 138th day of the year. The statement was concerning "Monkey Pox".

"Monkey Pox" 138 AO.

Something that needs to be discussed is that the government has long taught a perversion of evolution. A theory that was heavily promoted by Charles Darwin. Later in history Charles Dawson, interesting how close those names are, discovered an old skeleton that was given the name "piltdown man". It was accepted as true evidence for **41** years and used to promote the idea that white people began to evolve before other races. Piltdown was discovered on the day leaving 13 days left in the year, December 18th, 1912. Don't forget **41** is the *13th* prime, this being used as evidence for **41** years until proven as a complete fraud.

"Piltdown" *113* AO. **41** N.
"Science" **41** RN.
"Main Stream" *113* AO. **41** N.
"Bullshit" *113* RAO.
"Not True" *113* AO.
"Not Honest" *113* RAO.
113 a number receiving significance from Baba Kamma *113a*. "Jews may use lies ("subterfuges") to circumvent a Gentile."

"Conspiracy" 51 N. 57 RN.
"Piltdown Man" 51 N. 57 RN

Order Out of Chaos- In **1968** many foundations were set, future president George W. Bush graduated from Yale, the World Trade Center began construction before it fell 33 years later, 911 became the national emergency dialing code, MLK was assassinated. In 1968 the movie, "2001 A Space Odyssey" was released. It featured an A.I. taking control over a spacecraft attempting to kill all aboard. In 1968 the term "Coronavirus" was coined after ~ *'Dr. McIntosh's team discovered what is now known as OC43, another common human Coronavirus that still leads to respiratory infections today. The term "Coronavirus" was coined, based on how, under an electron microscope, its crown-like surface resembled the Sun's outer layer, called the corona.' April 11th, 2020. The Secret History of Coronavirus. Forbes.com.*

"Terror" **68** RAO.
"CIA" **68** RAO.
George Bush birthday is July 6th. including July 6th and counting to September 11th is exactly **68** days.

In response to the terror attacks the nation passed the "USA Patriot Act". To this day controversial and considered in many regards a violation of individual privacy. Wielding the slogan, 'war against terror', the act now allowed the government legal protection for; the tapping of domestic and international phones, increased penalties for terrorism crimes and an expanded list of what would qualify for terrorism charges, indefinite detainment without trial, the permission given to law enforcement to search property and records without a warrant, consent, or knowledge.~ *USA Patriot Act. Congress.gov.*

Shortly following these events the Patriots quarter back #11 Drew Bledsoe was sacked by Jets linebacker #57 Mo Lewis. The Jet ended the Patriot's career, leading to the rise of Tom Brady and a new era for the NFL. "When the human race learns to read the language of symbolism, a great veil will fall from the eyes of men. They shall then know truth and, more than that, they shall realize that from the beginning truth has been in the world unrecognized" – Manly P. Hall

"Terror" **68** RAO.
Jets #57 injures Patriots #11. 57+11=**68**

"USA Patriot Act" <u>47</u> N.
"Authority" <u>47</u> N.
"Government" <u>47</u> RN.

   Before continuing with the 9/11 and Coronavirus parallels lets observe how "terrorism" and **63** came together in 2020. On October 29th a woman was beheaded in France and two others were stabbed to death. October 29th is the day that leaves **63** days left in the year. ~ *France attack: Three killed in 'Islamist terrorist' stabbings. Bbc.com*. The attack being blamed on "Islamist extremists", who hold their most important prophet is Muhammad, who died at age **63**. It might be coincidence that Muhammad Ali died on **6-3**-2016 at the age of <u>74</u>. Of course 2016 is the **63**rd Triangular Number.

"Terrorism" **63** RN.

"Muhammad" <u>74</u> AO.
"Islamist Extremists" <u>74</u> N.

    The United States faced its biggest national emergency on **9/11.** The two 110 story towers that looked like a massive 11 standing next to each other came crumbling down on the 11th. What was the name of the first plane to hit on that day? It was Flight AA 11, A=1 so in numerology terms Flight 11 11, hits the giant 11 looking towers that are 110 stories tall on the 11th of September. Not to mention the random collapse of building <u>7</u>. With another plane involved on that day being Flight <u>77</u> which struck the Pentagon. The Pentagon is built on the **77th** meridian west of the globe. This all after the plane had been in the air for <u>77</u> minutes according to the **9/11** commission report. At 8:20 A.M. the flight took off, it later struck the Pentagon at 9:37 A.M. ~ *9/11 Commission Report. Govinfo.gov.* From 8:20 to 9:37 is undoubtedly <u>77</u> minutes.

"United States" <u>77</u> RN
"September Eleventh" <u>77</u> N.
"World Trade Center" <u>77</u> N.
"The Tower Of Babel" <u>77</u> RN.
Genesis **11:9** features the fall of The Tower of Babel.

The Biblical allegory can be drawn with the destruction of the two temples of the old testament which is remembered on the holiday of Tisha B'Av. Tisha B'Av is an annual fast day in Judaism, used to remember the disasters that occurred in Jewish history. Primarily the destruction of both Solomon's Temple by the Babylonian Empire and the destruction of the Second Temple by the Roman Empire. The destruction of the two temples, similar to the destruction of the two towers. Not to mention the other building to fall that day was building 7, Salomon Brothers building, reminding of the Temple of Solomon.

19 years after 2001 is 2020, and something to consider is that the moon is on a **19** year cycle, meaning that every **19** years the moon is in the exact same spot in relation to the Earth. In 2020 the government promised to protect us, from Covid-_ _. The 9/11 commission report also claims that there were **19** hijackers total on that day. (Pg. 46)

It's unsurprising to find out that before the bombing of Pearl Harbor, FDR had ignored reports of threats. Knowing congress would not condone war unless attacked. ~ *3 decades of warnings of an inevitable Japanese attack on Pearl Harbor went unheeded. Fox5dc.com.* I myself have visited the Pearl Harbor memorial and can attest that similar statements can be found there. The Pearl Harbor bombing took place on December 7th, a date that can be written as 12-7. The 9/11 attacks were compared to Pearl Harbor and many stated it was the worst thing to happen to America since. On 9/11 buildings 1, 2, and 7 were destroyed in New York during the attack. Today there stands a monument in place of the towers. The area where the towers stood is often referred to as "Ground Zero". Interesting as the nuclear weapons program code named 'Manhattan Project', is where the term 'Ground Zero' comes from. Definition: "Ground Zero"- the point on the surface of the earth or water directly below, directly above, or at which an atomic or hydrogen bomb explodes.

"Ground Zero" 127 RAO.
Buildings 1, 2, and 7 destroyed during the attacks.
The Pearl Harbor attacks took place on 12-7.

"Nuclear" 74 AO.
"Nuclear Weaponry" 74 N.
"Energy" 74 AO.

Many claim that Bush exacerbated the crisis by using it to further the military presence in the Middle East. Something that he knew congress would not condone unless there were fears of Weapons of Mass Destruction, WMDs. Many American citizens and foreign officials have questioned why the U.S. military didn't act or have prior intelligence of the incoming planned terrorist attack.
~ British official charges US "stood down" on 9/11.

wsws.org. The explanations given to the public felt rushed, incomplete, and couldn't hold up to reasoning. The most prominent example being when government officials claimed they had found the intact passports of the terrorist hijackers amongst the rubble of the towers. ~ *Officials said the two men, Khalid Al-Mihdhar and Nawaf Al-Hamzi, used their own names to buy airline tickets and board American Airlines Flight 77, which left Dulles International Airport and slammed into the Pentagon. Attorney General John Ashcroft said the investigation was "developing a kind of clarity" as the authorities pieced together the lives and recent movements of the 19 men and their ground-based accomplices.* **The passport of one hijacker was found today several blocks from the World Trade Center**, *prompting an intensive search for evidence in the area, Barry W. Mawn, who heads the F.B.I.'s New York office, said. The hijacker was not identified. September 16th, 2001. AFTER THE ATTACKS: THE INVESTIGATION; F.B.I. Was Seeking 2 of the Hijacking Suspects at the Time of the Attack. Nytimes.com.*

Mass Shootings- On December 14th, 2020 the first person in America to receive the Coronavirus "shot" was Sandra Lindsey, a black woman. In light of that date remember the Sandy Hook Shooting which took place on December 14th, 2017? Now the 14th of December leaves **17** days left in the year, then on the

17th of December, which is the pope's birthday, CNN put out an article claiming the U.S. Was now over **17** million people infected by the Coronavirus. Don't forget how the first televised vaccination in America featured a black woman and the government has already admitted to purposefully infecting black people with syphilis for research purposes.

"Shot" **17** N.
"Adam Lanza" **170** RAO.

After the Sandy Hook shooting was over, many news outlets reported how Adam Lanza weighed only 112 pounds. Probably to hint at the damage a small person can do with a gun. Let us see what Gematria can teach of the matter. Adam Lanza's birthday is April 22nd, April 22nd is the 112th day of the year. A is the 1st letter and L is the 12th. Thus 112 pound Adam Lanza who's initials are 1.12 reportedly born on the 112th day on the year shot up the school.

The "Dunblane" massacre caused the U.K. to lose their gun rights when a man shot up a school in Scotland. This mass shooting took place March 13th, 1996. Now March 13th is the **73rd** day of the year during leap years, and the year 1996 was indeed a leap year. Later the families of the Sandy Hook school shooting victims got a **$73,000,000** settlement.

"Dunblane" **73** AO.

March 13th is the **73rd** day of the year in leap years.

   'Luckily' New York has just passed a similar statute that Connecticut used to sue Remington. Not long after were the reports of a shooting at a Tops market place in Buffalo, New York. The young shooter was armed with expensive armor and after market weapon mods, that media outlets estimated was worth a minimum of $10,000. Begging the question how did this young person afford all this warfare equipment? The shooting in "Buffalo", New York came **63** days before the start of the NFL training camps. The 2022-2023 year will be the Buffalo Bills **63rd** season in the NFL. The mayor of Buffalo, Byron Brown, was **63** years old at the time of the shooting. The only NFL team to officially visit the memorial of the shooting was the Tampa Bay Buccaneers. At the same time Biden was receiving praise for passing the 'BRADY BILL'. Tying back into the theme of racism as the bill made lynching a federal hate crime. The media reported that the shooter of the Tops market was motivated by "racism", even though the video shown to the public shows the first person he shot was a white woman.

"Buffalo" **63** AO.

"Racism" **63** AO.

The store reopened **63** days after the shooting, the same day NFL training camps opened for the season.

On May 24th, 2022 in Uvalde, Texas it was reported that a young gunman had entered a school and killed <u>19 students and 2 teachers</u>. The 18 year old shooter, "Salvador Ramos", had celebrated his birthday 8 days before the shooting. (**4+4=8**). The police had the classroom he was in surrounded but had refused to attempt to rush the shooter. There were 19 police that waited out in the hallway. The first victim to have their name released was the **44** year old, **4th** grade teacher Eva Mireles. The number 4 is associated with death being that in Japanese the word for 'death' and the word for '4' are pronounced the same way. '4' is spelled 四 and 'Death' is spelled 死, the English Transliteration for both is 'Shi'. From governor of Texas Greg Abbott's November 13, 2021 birthday to the date of the shooting in Uvalde, Texas was exactly <u>192</u> days later. Then **4** days after the shooting, Kamala Harris called for an "assault weapons" ban. Of course completely by coincidence.

"Assault Weapons" <u>192</u>
<u>19 Students 2 Teachers killed</u>
<u>192 days after Texas governor's birthday</u>

"Salvador Ramos" **193** RAO.

193 is the **44**th Prime Number in sequence of Primes.
"Kill" **44** AO.
"Execution" **44** N.
"Shooting" **44** N.

   As Americans celebrated the 4th of July, 2022 a gunman posted on the high ground of a market place in Highland Park, Illinois shot down at a crowd. He escaped from the scene causing police to declare an "active shooter" situation. Later he was arrested and the details of the event were reported to the public. The Highland Park area was reported to have an above average "Jewish" population. The shooter had reportedly been told to leave a synagogue by a local rabbi a few weeks prior to the shooting. The shooter had also posted multiple videos depicting violence to YouTube were he promoted himself as a "rapper". When the media released the image of the shooter, prominently featured on his face was tattooed the number "47".

July 4th can be written 4/7 or 7/4
"Active Shooter" **74** RN.
"Rapper" **74** AO.
"Killing" **74** AO.
"Jewish" **74** AO.
"Holiday" **74** AO.
"Fourth of Jew Lie" **74** N.
"Independence Day" **74** N.

On **October 1ˢᵗ**, 2017 there was a mass shooting that took place in Las Vegas. The gunman posted in his suite inside the "Mandalay Bay Casino", and shot at a crowd of people enjoying a concert. The headline performer of the concert was **Jason Aldean**. Notice J is the 10ᵗʰ letter and A is the 1ˢᵗ, like the date October 1ˢᵗ would be written **10/1**. Fox News reported that 'during the last song of Aldean's set, *"When She Says Baby"*, shots started ringing out.' At the end of the shooting, *59* people were declared dead. Jason Aldean's birthday is February 28ᵗʰ, the *59ᵗʰ* day of the year. In the year 2017, the holiday Yom Kippur had ended the day prior to the shooting. Yom Kippur is regarded as the day to seek atonement for your sins. The gunman decided to shoot up 'Sin City' the day after Yom Kippur concluded.

"Mandalay Bay Casino" **101** RN.
J **10** A **1**,
Jason Aldean concert headline, **10/1** date

"When She Says Baby" *59* N.
"Jason" *59* AO.
Jason Aldean's birthday, February 28ᵗʰ, the *59ᵗʰ* day of year.
59 people declared dead.

"The Day Of Atonement" *74* N.

"Active Shooter" *74* RN.

Shaping The Nation- With regards to the major repetitive ritual that took place in 2019 with the arrest and eventual suicide of "Jeffery Epstein". He was arrested on July 6th, the 178th day of the year by, the FBI-NYPD Crimes Against Children Task Force. He was charged with the crime of sex trafficking "minors". "Jeffery Edward Epstein" was charged on July 8th in "Brooklyn New York", which was **34** days before his August 10th death. Many under the impression that he didn't commit "suicide" but was "murdered". August 10th is the 222nd day of the year, the man died with many believing he was a "pedophile". Notice he died *163* days before his birthday, not contrary to his name which sums to *163*. If you look at the prisoner number given to Epstein you'll see it is "76318-054", 7+6+3+1+8+0+5+4=**34**.

"Jeffery Epstein" *163* AO.
Died *163* days before birthday
"Jeffery Edward Epstein" 322 RAO.
"Brooklyn, New York" 223 AO.
Died on the 222nd day of the year, also the 223rd in leap years, August 10th.

Jeffery Epstein" 163 AO. (163 is the *38th* Prime in sequence of Primes.)

"Murder" **34** N. *83* RAO. *38* RN.
"Suicide" **34** N.
"Epstein" **34** N. *38* RN.
"Minors" **34** N. *38* RN.

Corey Lewandowski reportedly tested positive for covid 56 days after his September 18th birthday, the news being reported on November 12th, 2020. That same day, November 12th, CNN put out an article titled *"'Dejected' Trump continues to waffle over waging baseless election fight".~ cnn.com.* Notice how <u>they</u> put the word Dejected in parentheses. This was during the headlines of Trump 'suffering' from getting covid. The elderly overweight man survived the virus with no long term effect.

"Coronavirus" **56** N.
"Dejected" **56** AO.

"Ben Carson" also reportedly tested positive for "Covid" on November 9th, 2020 which was exactly **53** days after his September 18th birthday. *~Ben Carson tests positive for covid-19. Nbcnews.com*

"Ben Carson" **53** RN
"Covid" **53** AO.

On August 3rd, 2020 a day ripe for a murder ritual being that the day can be written **8-3** or **3-8**, John

Hume died at the age of 83. He was famous for brokering the "Good Friday" agreement. The date of the agreement was signed was on April 10th 1988, a date that can be written 10-4.

With all these 38, 83 connections the older generations may remember the song by the band 'The Police', Murder by Numbers, on their album 'synchronicity' in 1983. Also connecting is that the movie 'Murder by Numbers' only uses the numbers 8 and 3 in the title to replace the B and the E. The main actress in the movie is "Sandra Bullock"

"Good Friday" 104 AO.
"Murder" 83 RAO. 38 RN.
"Sandra Bullock" 83 RN

A major ritual that occurred in 2020 was the televised killing of a black man "George Perry Floyd". He was pulled out of his car by a police cruiser with the number 803 on the back. Then after being dragged into clear view of the intersection of 38th street he was "murdered". He was killed by "park" "police" when the officer put his knee on the "neck" of Floyd who's official cause of death was "asphyxia due to neck and back compression".

"asphyxia due to neck and back compression" 383 AO.
"Murder" 83 RAO. 38 RN.

"Killing" **38** N.
"Death" **38** AO. *20* N.

Notice the *20* in "death" as *2020* has been a year a mass death due to Coronavirus. George Floyd was initially confronted for a fake $*20* bill. This happened weeks after the $*20* bill featuring Harriet Tubman would be delayed from release. To date the Harriet Tubman bill has still not been released.

This was all preceded with the NFL controversy of African American players kneeling during the National Anthem. Shockingly, in the video he is heard crying out "I can't breathe". All this reportedly because he paid with a fake $*20* bill, in the year 2020 where the $20 bill featuring Harriet Tubman was supposed to debut. After this there was a radical rise in news coverage around the group "Black Lives Matter" In light of this event "NASCAR" dedicated car number 43 to Black Lives Matter after the death of "George Floyd". Then on the date June 10th, 2020 NASCAR banned the Confederate Flag from their events, a date that can be written *10-6.* Many watched the "riots" on TV and feared the outbreak of a "Civil War" or "Race War". In light of it being the year of the 46th presidential election notice George Floyd died at age 46.

"George Floyd" **43** RN.

"Civil War" **43** N.
"NASCAR" 106 RAO. **43** RN.

"Floyd" 26 N.
"Park" 26 RN.
"Riot" 26 N.

"Black" 106 RAO.
"Black Lives Matter" 106 RN.
"I Can't Breathe" 106 AO.

"Race War" *33* N.
"Police" *33* N.
"KKK" *33* AO.
"Chauvin" *33* N.

The verdict finding Chauvin guilty came on April 20th, 2021. A date that is written **4-20,** with The number **42** most notably associated with African Americans. Chauvin was sentenced to 22.5 years in prison. Floyd was killed on May 25th, 2020, including the day that he died in the count, it was exactly 225 days after his October 14th, 2019 birthday. Not unrelated on May 27th, 2022, just 2 days after the death of George Floyd, Catholic diocese in Minnesota paid out $22.5 million for sexual abuse. ~ *Catholic diocese in Minnesota to pay sexual abuse victims $22.5m. Theguardian.com.* Tying into the story paraded in the news cycles about

George Floyd and his elementary school teachers. The mainstream media quoted Floyd's former teacher, '**Wanynel Sexton**', who taught at Fredrick Douglass Elementary for 24 years'. ~ *George Floyd's second-grade teacher shares an essay about his wanting to be a Supreme Court justice. Nydailynews.com.*

Seeing that Race War and Police sum to *33* lets look at one of the most significant events that sparked race riots across L.A. California. The event being the March 3rd beating of "Rodney King" by the "L.A. PD". March 3rd being a date that is written *3-3*. Rodney King eventually passed away from his injuries at the age of 47. He died on June 17th 2012, <u>76</u> days after his April 2nd birthday. Notice his birthday can be written **4-2**. The 76 also stands out in light of the Million Man March taking place on the day leaving <u>76</u> days left in the year. After he was "beat" L.A. Had the most notorious "riot" to date. After the death of Michael Brown the media put out the picture of the police officer Darren Wilson, who shot Michael Brown wearing a Blues Hockey shirt that prominently showed the number **42**.

"L.A. PD" *33* AO.
"Police" *33* N.
"Race War" *33* N.
"KKK" *33* AO.

"The Police" **42** RN.
"Bravo Mike" **42** N.
Police code for Black Male, (B)ravo (M)ike)

"Beat" 26 RN.
"Riot" 26 N.

   The death of "Breonna Taylor" was also a big
event in the minds of the masses. It was reported that
police entered and shot her dead while serving a
search warrant. The shooting took place March 13th,
2020 however, "Brett Hankison" who shot her, was
not indicted until September 23rd, 2020. The distance
between those dates is exactly **195** days, observe the
Gematria value for the cop's name below. The main
legal battle behind the incident was whether or not
police could serve a "no knock warrant" in this case.

"Brett Hankison" **195** RAO.

"Breonna Taylor" 191 RAO. 191 is the 43rd Prime
Number in sequence of Primes.
"Murdered" 43 N.
"Killing" *38* N. 43 RN.
"R.I.P" 43 AO. *38* RAO.

"No Knock Warrant" *83* RN.
"Murder" *83* RAO.

World Wars- We will begin by looking at what modern political analysis experts are declaring to be the start of WW3. Of course this brings us to the emerging "Russian Ukraine war". After moving military forces to be stationed around the boarders of Ukraine on February 22nd, 2022, Russia decided to officially invade Ukraine on February 24th, 2022. The official invasion date may signify something quite telling. Adding the numerology from that date gives us the total of **68**. This date numerology total is interesting because of the fact that it relates not only back to WW2 but also WW1 starting dates. The 1st World War began on 7/28/1914 with Russia coming to Serbia's defense after Austria declared war, the system of alliances effectively drawing in all of Europe. The 2nd World War had the starting date of 1/9/1939 with the German invasion of Poland.

"Russian Ukraine War" 222 AO.
Troops positioned on 2/22/22.
2/24/2022 Russia invades Ukraine
2+24+20+22= **68**
7/28/1914 Austria declares war on Serbia
7+28+19+14= **68**
1/9/1939 Germany invades Poland
9+1+19+39= **68**
"Terror" **68** RAO.

One of the most popular written works of all time on the subject of war is "Art of War", attributed to Sun Zhu. However it is interesting to note that there is no historical proof that a, 'Sun Zhu', ever existed. What is documented, is that the first translation to English of Art of War was done by, Roger Copeland Ames, an American Anglican priest. What's a priest doing reading about the art of war? As mentioned earlier the "Jesuit" order, esteemed for their ability to infiltrate and play sides against each other, had great influence even back then in the early 1900's. Recently Activision was purchased by Bill Gates, they had released a video game set in a fictional Ukraine. The game is titled Call of Duty "War zone". Sadly, all these rumors of war come on the back of the pandemic. The pandemic was declared in March 2020, coming **102** years after the declaration of the Spanish Flu pandemic in 1918.

2020-1918= **102** Years Later
"War Zone" **102** AO.
"World War" **102** RAO.

Mathew 10:34
"I have not come to bring peace, but a sword"
181 RN.
181 is the *42nd* Prime in sequence of Prime Numbers.
"War" *42* AO.
"World War" *42* N.

Enlightened thinkers throughout history and around the globe have warned against the nature of warfare and its ultimate harm upon humanity. Such as Martin Luther King Jr., who was murdered in relation to his speaking out against war. But in the current American system many young men and woman without a clear path of receiving a college education are enticed to serve the military for this and other benefits. Focusing on the 18 year olds the government seeks to stock its mercenary forces with the trusting students generally sourced from public education establishments. In recent years federal laws have banned the purchase of tobacco and nicotine products for 18 year olds. The majority of states maintain that to gamble and purchase liquor the purchaser must be 21. However if enlisted one would be able to defile the human rights and national sovereignty of others, as a "mercenary" of freedom. One thing is impossible to deny, that is that, "war" and "world wars" have often been used as a means of "population control". The Georgia Guide Stones were recently demolished but originally the monument laid out laws in multiple languages for all to observe. The monument was originally placed on 22/3/1980. One of the laws given is "Maintain humanity under 500,000,000 in perpetual balance with nature.". Realize the current estimated population on earth is 7.7 billion.

"Population Control" <u>223</u> RAO.
"Desecration Of Human Life" <u>223</u> AO.
223 is the <u>48</u>th Prime Number in sequence of Primes.
"Mercenary" <u>48</u> N.
"World War" <u>48</u> RN.

"Military" **44** N.
"Private" **44** RN.
"Officer" **44** N.
"Trooper" **44** N.
"Soldier" **44** RN.
"Kill" **44** AO.

April 4th, 1967
"A few years ago there was a shining moment in that struggle. It seemed as if there was a real promise of hope for the poor—both black and white—through the poverty program. There were experiments, hopes, new beginnings. Then came the buildup in Vietnam and I watched the program broken and eviscerated as if it were some idle political plaything of a society gone mad on war, and I knew that America would never invest the necessary funds or energies in rehabilitation of its poor so long as adventures like Vietnam continued to draw men and skills and money like some demonic destructive suction tube. So I was increasingly compelled to see the war as an enemy of the poor and to attack it as such.

Perhaps the more tragic recognition of reality took place when it became clear to me that the war was doing far more than devastating the hopes of the poor at home. It was sending their sons and their brothers and their husbands to fight and to die in extraordinarily high proportions relative to the rest of the population. We were taking the black young men who had been crippled by our society and sending them eight thousand miles away to guarantee liberties in Southeast Asia which they had not found in southwest Georgia and East Harlem. So we have been repeatedly faced with the cruel irony of watching Negro and white boys on TV screens as they kill and die together for a nation that has been unable to seat them together in the same schools. So we watch them in brutal solidarity burning the huts of a poor village, but we realize that they would never live on the same block in Detroit. I could not be silent in the face of such cruel manipulation of the poor.

My third reason moves to an even deeper level of awareness, for it grows out of my experience in the ghettoes of the North over the last three years—especially the last three summers. As I have walked among the desperate, rejected and angry young men I have told them that Molotov cocktails and rifles would not solve their problems. I have tried to offer them my deepest compassion while maintaining my conviction that social change comes most meaningfully through nonviolent action. But they asked—and rightly so—what about Vietnam? They asked if our own nation wasn't using massive doses of violence to solve its problems, to bring about the changes it wanted. Their questions hit home, and I knew that I could never again raise my voice against the violence of the oppressed in the ghettos without having first spoken clearly to the greatest purveyor of violence in the world today—my own government. For the sake of those boys, for the sake of this government, for the sake of hundreds of thousands trembling under our violence, I cannot be silent."

- Martin Luther King Jr. 'Beyond Vietnam: A Time to Break Silence' April 4th, 1967

Abortion- On **May 2nd**, 2022 many news outlets reported there was a leak, coming from the supreme court, that Roe v. Wade would soon be overturned. Before proceeding realize that May 2nd is the **122nd** day of the year. Roe v Wade was officially overturned on June 24th, 2022. Counting from May 2nd to June 24th it is a span of 53 days, which also calculates as **1** month and **22** days.

"Abortion" 122 RAO.

Norma McCorvey took the name 'Jane Roe', similar to generic name 'John Doe' during the trial. While at first glance the name change seems to suggest that she may be expressing that this is an issue for everybody. However when you consider that 'roe' is defined as: The mass of eggs contained in the ovaries of a female fish or shellfish, typically including the ovaries themselves, especially when ripe and used as food. Also phonetically involved is the theme of rowing not to mention the opponent Wade, both associated with water. Meanwhile these decisions were to set precedents pertaining to fetuses in the amniotic fluid. The ruling for Roe v Wade came on January 22nd, 1973. Expressing the date shorthand would give us **1-22**. Now, counting from Norma McCorvey's September 22nd, 1972 birthday to the date of the decision for Roe v. Wade, January 22nd, 1973 is exactly a span of **122** days later.

"Abortion" **122** RAO.

Following the overturning many pro-choice minded people protested and demonstrated their frustrations. The majority of demonstrators wearing the color "green". Many pundits argue this stems from Marta Alanis, founder of 'Catholics for the Right to Decide'. She had proposed wearing green scarfs as a "symbol of hope, health, and life.' at the 18th National Women's Meeting in Argentina, 2003.

What can Gematria teach into this symbolic representation? While we touched on the "heart chakra" earlier (pg. 72), here society displays the acting out of symbolism. Abortion has long been one of the most divisive issues in "America". With the federal government differing the authority to states on the matter, the heart strings of many were pulled into action, wearing their green clothing.

"Your Heart" **49** RN.
"Emotional" **49** RN.
"Green" **49** AO.
"Washington" **49** N.
Washington is the only state with a Green flag.
Norma McCorvey died on February 18th, the **49th** day of the year.
"Heart Chakra" **94** AO. **49** N.
"Abortion" **94** AO

Transgenderism- The biggest culture shock of the twenty first century is undoubtedly the rise in transgenderism and the associated LGBTQ movement. Homosexuality is a part of human history, there have always been those that thought themselves born as the wrong gender. However, never before have surgeries that alter the human body been so accessible. Making this point an issue was the U.S. government deciding to fund sex change operations if military personnel wanted to do so. January 25th, 2021 Biden passed an executive order that covers sex change costs for active service members and veterans. The executive order is estimated to cost tax payers a minimum of $100,000 per a year. ~ *Transgender surgery is now free for military, thanks to Biden executive order. Washingtonexecutive.com*

Unfortunately the suicide rate is even higher for those who go through life transgender. This should make one question: Why does the government media promote a lifestyle that statistically promotes suicide in young people?

Yahoo: **The suicide rate among transgender teens is shockingly high** September 12th, 2018.
"The numbers were much higher for transgender or nonbinary teens: Slightly more than half of transgender male teens (50.8 percent) said they had tried to kill themselves, while 41.8 percent of teens who identified as neither male nor female, and nearly 30 percent of transgender female teens said the same thing. About 28 percent of teens who identified themselves as "questioning" their sexual orientation also said they had tried to kill themselves."

"Christine Jorgensen" was the first American to become widely known for undergoing a sex change operation. They had a career as a successful actress, singer, and recording artist. Their transition was the first to be discussed by the public and brought the idea of gender reassignment to light. Jorgensen encouraged others who felt the same to alter their birth certificates and change their names. They were born on the date, May 30th, 1926 and died on the date, May 3rd, 1989. Notice how both dates are written **5-30** and **5-3**.

"Gender" **53** AO.
"Transgender" **53** N.

There were multiple head lines about University of "Pennsylvania" transgender swimmer, "Lia Thomas". It's somehow an ongoing debate if someone who has changed their "gender" surgically, should be allowed to compete with the gender they have transitioned to. Lia Thomas, a perfect example of this being *6'4"* tall with broad shoulders. The headlines came on February 22, 2022 which is the **53rd** day of the year.

They are *6'4"* tall.
"Transgender" **53** N. *64* RN.
"Pennsylvania" **53** N. *64* RN.
"Gender" **53** AO. <u>35</u> N.
"Lia Thomas" <u>35</u> N.

A comedian seen as a symbol of outspokenness against the transgender movement is Dave Chappelle. Stating notoriously, "Every human being in this room, every human being on Earth had to pass through the legs of a woman to be on Earth, that is a fact," Chappelle says in the special. "Now I am not saying that to say that trans women aren't women. I am just saying that those pussies that they got … you know what I mean?" I'm not saying it's not pussy, but that's like beyond pussy or impossible pussy."

Following those statements Dave Chappelle was attacked while performing on May 3rd, 2022. He was performing on the "Hollywood Bowl" stage. The attacker was ambushed by security and barely got ahold of Chappelle. It was later revealed that the attacker's arm was broken and that they were transgender. On Chappelle's first appearance back following the attack, he exclaimed 'that was a "trans man"!'

May 3rd, a date written **5/3**
"Hollywood Bowl" *64* N. **53** RN.
"Trans Man" **53** RN.
"Gender" **53** AO.
"Transgender" **53** N. *64* RN.
"Dave Chappelle" 241 RAO. 241 is the **53rd** Prime Number in sequence of Primes.

Another transgender story announced that Mj Rodriguez had won a golden globe for their part in the TV show "Pose". The impact of this being that Mj Rodrigues is the first transgender actor/actress to receive a "Golden Globe".

"Pose" 53 RN.
"Golden Globe" 53 N.
"Gender" 53 AO.
"Transgender" 53 N.

On March 29th, 2021 Time Magazine put Elliot Page on the cover of their magazine. This made them the first "transgender" person to appear on the cover of Time. Caitlyn Jenner had been on the cover of "Vanity Fair", but these headlines about "Time Magazine" seemed just as widespread.

3/29/2021. 3+29+21= **53**
"Transgender" **53** N.
"Gender" **53** AO.
"Vanity Fair" **53** N.

"Caitlyn Jenner" 201 RAO.
"Time Magazine" 201 RAO.
"Gender Studies" 201 RAO.

Bruce Jenner made shock and headlines when they said 'for all intensive purposes I am a woman'.

"Jenner" definitely helped usher in the topic of transgenderism into the main stream when the public witnessed the conversion from a man to a "woman". For those that wanted more insight into the madness, as the public is rather fond of the Kardashian family, there was a TV show made titled "I am Cait".

"Jenner" *66* AO.
"Woman" *66* AO.

"I Am Cait" 56 AO.
"Mind Control" 56 N.

A story that made national headlines on June 6th, 2022 was that the Carolina Panthers had hired a transgender "woman" for their cheer squad. "Justine Lindsay" was reported as the 'first openly transgender cheerleader in the NFL'. The cheer squad they signed with has the title of the "Carolina Panthers TopCats". These headlines came 97 days before the season opener for the Carolina Panthers, September 11th, 2022.

"Carolina Panthers TopCats" 97 N.
97 days before season opener.
"Justine Lindsay" 56 N.
"I Am Cait" 56 AO.
"Mind Control" 56 N.

"Carolina" **53** RN.
"Transgender" **53** N.
"Gender" **53** AO.

"Woman" *66* AO.
"Jenner" *66* AO.
6/6 date of the headlines

   The modern consensus by and large seems to be accepting of transgenderism. A nation that prides itself on freedom has no issues with new 'freedoms' being acknowledged as long as no others are tarnished. However, overwhelmingly there is public outrage over the use of LGBTQ themes and characters being used in children's media. Many parents wish for these ideas not to be intermingling with their kids developing personality. As stated before it is actually statistically provable these ideas bring more mental and physical harm to children. But in response the LGBTQ argument is that if they are to have equal human rights they deserve to have their ideas out in the 'free market' of ideas. Gallup polls considers the percentage of the population that identify as LGBTQ is approximately ~ 7.1% of the American population. However the public is becoming alarmed because the themes and characters promoting the LGBTQ agendas appear in far more than 7% of modern media.

The concept that gay and trans couples can have children has become feasible through adopting and even sperm donation. However the success and acceptance rates are not 100%. Funds and legal paper work required also make these options a hassle for straight and gay couples alike. Hinting towards the generally accepted fact that gay couples can not reproduce together, nor can someone who surgically changes their gender reproduce. Making these permanent life altering decisions available to children could have devastating effects, unknown to current society. For those that claim there is no agenda and that society is naturally progressing this way, simply look to the statue placed outside the Arkansas state capitol by the Satanic Church, showing Baphomet, a hermaphrodite god, with a male child and female child looking up to them.

"Baphomet" 35 N.
"Gender" 35 N.

Forgive me but I would be remiss to end this section without presenting the language modern intellectuals use on the issue of transgenderism and religion;
A professor of theological ethics at Villanova:
'Since Jesus had no human biological father, and since God, his heavenly Father, lacks a body, then Jesus was a man who likely had no Y chromosome.

Would this not make Jesus more like a transgender person than a cis-gender one? We could grant Jesus a Y chromosome, but then we would have to assign his virgin mother Mary one as well. Either way, the miracle of sex-less conception suggests that Jesus can qualify as a "real man" only if Mary qualifies as something less than a "real woman."' ~ Jesus Was Transgender? I Thought He Was Gay. Nationalreview.com.

We operate on the Gregorian calendar named after a Pope, the English language was standardized by catholic influence and adaptation, and the most popular religion in the western world and seemingly abroad was created by a Roman council. Did this some how influence our inherited historical understanding and recording of events? Is there any hint that the victors are rewriting history? Think back to the most famous quote in Orwell's '1984',
"The one who controls the past, controls the future, the one who controls the present, controls the past."

SPORTS & CELEBRITY
"You couldn't have scripted it any better"

Perhaps the most dangerous profession in America is to be a celebrity, with the **27** club claiming world famous members and rappers dropping dead seemingly every month. Ask yourself who would want to be one if it wasn't for the love of money and fame that controls the minds of the masses. These celebrities whether aware or not are often given performer names corresponding with their archetype, birthday, and eventual televised death to come. Not contrary with "Kobe Bean Bryant" who's most impactful moment on the court came when he scored 81 points. Sports athletes in the leagues outwardly admit they are there for entertainment and business, not the pure spirit of competition.

"Kobe Bean Bryant" 81 RN.
"Ritual" 81 AO. **27** N. 81 RAO.

SPORTS- Following the death of Kobe, the L.A. Lakers won the 2020 NBA Finals, on "Father Daughter Day" October 11th, 2020. The sick joke of course being the "Kobe Bryant" died with his daughter in the helicopter crash. This finals win headed by "king" Lebron James was the Lakers 17th championship. Laughable when you notice that

Lebron re-signed for $154 million with the Lakers on July 1st, a date written 1-7, coincidence?

Not unrelated is that the day before Kobe died Lebron past him in points scored all time, moving Kobe to 4th place. The number 4 is associated with death being that in Japanese the word for 'death' and the word for '4' are pronounced the same way. 4 is spelled 四 and Death is spelled 死, the English transliteration for both is 'Shi'. Again compounding with the facts, "kill" sums to 44 AO, the "execution" of MLK for speaking out against the "military" on April 4th, a date written 4-4.

When Lebron won the finals he accumulated a total of **172** playoff wins, like "Father Daughter Day" sums to **172**. Lebron James left Miami and went back to Cleveland **172** days after his December 30th birthday. Notice that 12+30 = **42**, Lebron being arguably the most famous black athlete in history with the **42** stamped on his birthday, and his name "Lebron James". It was reported that Kobe's helicopter crashed in **4200** block, even though pictures and video coverage showed the wreckage in a grass field. The record being **4-2** of this years finals series. The Lakers went 4-1 in every series of the playoffs except the finals, like "Kobe Bryant" sums to 41. When wearing their 'Black Mamba Jerseys' the Lakers were undefeated in the playoffs. That is until "game five" in the finals when they lost, making their playoff record in those jerseys, 4-1. Earlier in the year George Floyd was killed in Minnesota, which is the original home of the Lakers franchise.

"Father Daughter Day" **172** AO.
"L.A." <u>41</u> RAO.
"King" <u>41</u> AO.
"Kobe Bryant" <u>41</u> N.

"Lebron James" **42** N.
"Slavery" **42** RN.
"Nigger" **42** N.
"Tuskegee" **42** RN.

Earlier in the year on March 11th, 2020 the World Health Organization officially declared Corona Virus a 'pandemic'. A date that could be written 11-3. On that same day the NBA put a hold on the leagues play due to the virus. The Utah Jazz were reported to have an outbreak of covid among their players. Which reminds, before the virus was in full swing ask yourself. What was the biggest headline in the few months before the pandemic declaration? Well if you're a fan of "The National Basketball Association" you remember the death of "Kobe Bryant" at age **41**, on January 26th, 2020. "Kobe Bean Bryant" had his best game when he scored <u>*81*</u> points in his 666th game of his career in what was an obvious "ritual". Kobe played his final career game against the "Utah Jazz". In 2017, Kobe Bryant put out an animated film based on his 2015 retirement speech. The film is titled "Dear Basketball".

"Apocalypse" *113* AO. **41** N.
"Kobe Bryant" *113* AO. **41** N. (Dead at age **41**)
"Dear Basketball" *113* AO. **41** N.
"Michael Jordan" *113* AO.
"The National Basketball Association" *113* N.
"Utah Jazz" *113* AO.

"Kobe Bean Bryant" *81* RN
"Ritual" *81* AO. *81* RAO.

The actor Chadwick Boseman who's birthday was November 9th, 1977 died at the age **42**. He was the main actor in the movie about "Jackie" Robinson titled "**42**". The day he died August 28th, 2020 was 'Jackie Robinson Day' in the MLB. August 28th is also the birthday of Jack Kirby who is the co-author of Black Panther. Chadwick's most famous movie performance was in the movie 'Black Panther' where he played the character "T'challa". In the 2020 season the L.A. Dodgers, who acquired the star player "Mookie Bets" on February 4th a date that can be written **4-2,** won the MLB World Series on the day of Jackie Robinson's funeral, October 27th, 2020. The series went a total of 6 games thus the final record was L.A. Winning **4-2**. The Dodgers hadn't won a World Series in 32 years and they had a total of 32 runs in the six games. Remember the 32 RAYS on the sun in the Jesuit logo. If you include the Rays runs, who scored 22, 32+22=54, like "baseball" sums to 54 AO and RN. (9 innings x 6 outs total per an inning= *54* total outs in a game) "Baseball" also sums to <u>18</u> which each team given 9 innings to bat, meaning 9×2=18. A baseball is bound together by **108** hand-woven stitches through the cowhide leather. The sport purposefully named with Gematria in mind. Another piece of the puzzle is that Jackie Robinson was in the U.S. Army—a second lieutenant assigned to the 761st Tank Battalion, the 'Black Panthers'.

"Baseball" *54* AO. <u>18</u> N. *54* RN
"Major League" **108** AO.

"Jackie" **<u>42</u>** RN.
Jackie wore the #42 and Chadwick Boseman stared in the movie titled **<u>42</u>**.
"T'challa" **<u>42</u>** RN.
"Mookie Bets" **<u>42</u>** N.
"Jigga Boo" **<u>42</u>** RN
"Slavery" **<u>42</u>** RN.
"Nigger" **<u>42</u>** N

   The star of the movie 'Goodfellas', Ray Liotta died May 26th, 2022. He was currently filming a movie in the Dominican Republic at the town of "Santo

Domingo". May 26th is the 146th day of the year. On May 26th, 2022 the MLB teams the Reds and Cubs played each other with the final score being 20-5. Scheduled for August, 11th, 2022 the Reds and Cubs will play in the 'Field of Dreams Game'. Ray Liotta acted the character "Shoeless Joe Jackson" in the movie Field of Dreams. The name of his character equals **205** using the alphabetical order, the score of the two teams on the date of his death was **20-5**. ~ *Cubs vs. Reds – Game Summary – May 26th, 2022. Espn.com.*

"Shoeless Joe Jackson" **205** AO.

"Santo Domingo" 146 AO.
Dead May 26th the 146th day of the year.
GoodFellas has a 2 Hour 26 Minute run time, a total of 146 Minutes.

   John Madden was made world famous with his name branded on to one of the most successful video game series of all time, Madden NFL. Though many other companies have tried to get a foot in the door with the "National Football League", Madden has always been the unanimous leader in sales. He passed away on December 28th, 2021 with the headlines reading *"NFL Legend John Madden" dead at* **85**.

"NFL Legend John Madden" **85** RN.
"National Football League" **85** N.
Dead at age **85**.

The 2015 NFL super bowl all came down to one play. It was 2nd and 1, Russell Wilson dropped back and took his 21st pass attempt of the game. The pass was intercepted by #21 of the defense. As #21 was tackled after the interception there were 21 seconds left on the clock. The super bowl was played on the date February 1st or 2-1, 2015. Tom Brady entered the game with 21 career playoff wins.

7 days before the outbreak of war in <u>Ukraine</u>, the Rams had won the NFL super bowl for the 2021-2022 season. At the time of the game the Rams head coach was engaged to <u>Ukrainian</u> model Veronika Khomyn. Note that the zodiac sign of Aries is symbolized by a ram and in the ancient Greek myths, Aries was the god of war.

After the rams had won their championship we saw the WARriors win the NBA championship for the 2021-2022 season. The Warriors played the Celtics in the finals. The two teams hadn't played each other in the finals since the year 19**64**. The Warriors picked up their **4**th win of the series in game **6**. The date of game 6 coming on June 16th, 2022. The date numerology being (6+16+20+22= **64**).

The Rams have blue and yellow jerseys, the Warriors have blue and yellow jerseys, the Ukraine flag features the colors blue and yellow. The 2021-2022 NHL Stanley Cup winner was the Colorado Avalanche, their logo is a red, white, and blue A. The 2021-2022 MLB World Series was won by the Atlanta Braves, their logo is a red, white, and blue A. Red, white, and blue are the colors featured on the Russian flag.

Alex Smith had a brutal leg injury after a hit by #**99** J.J. Watt on November 18th, 2018. Alex Smith would return to the NFL exactly **99** weeks later for the team formerly known as the "Redskins". Alex Smith wears number "<u>eleven</u>". On that same day as he returned, October <u>11</u>th, 2020, the quarterback of the Cowboys, Dak Prescott broke his leg in the prime time night game. Think about it, Redskins and Cowboys one quarterback returns from a leg injury and their rival team's quarterback leaves with a leg injury, as above so below, as below so above.

"Redskins" **99** AO.
"Eleven" **99** RAO.

On October 25th, 2020 the pope announced the appointment of the first black 'cardinal'. On that same night the NFL Cardinals were rescheduled to play in the prime time slot. The Cardinals wore their all black uniforms and of course, won the game with the score being 37-34, a total of *71* points. The Cardinals then became **5-2**, aligning with the fact that the 2020-2021 super bowl would be **52** days after the pope's birthday. The date this ritual took place was 105 days before the super bowl.

"Catholic" *71* AO. *35* N.
"Phoenix, AZ" *35* RN.
"Pope" **52** AO.
"Arizona Cardinals" 105 RN.

   During the mass power outages in Houston, Texas J.J. Watt was signed to the Arizona Cardinals. Leaving Texas, the state known for its oil industries and coming to Arizona the solar energy capitol. For further symbolism look at his last name. A watt is a unit of measurement dealing with electricity.
   Not to be out done Deshaun Watson made headlines for inappropriate behavior towards an Asian woman at a massage parlor. The following week March 16th, 2021 there was multiple shootings at massage parlors in Georgia that made the national headlines. Deshaun Watson is originally from Georgia. Shortly after on March 31st, 2021 the national news made sure everyone saw a large black man push over an elderly Asian lady and proceed to kick her for seemingly no reason. This security camera footage coming the day after the trial began

for the police officers involved with the George Floyd incident, one of the officers is Asian. March 31st is the **90th** day of the year. Shortly after this event, on April 14th, 2021 the masters tournament had its first ever Asian champion. ~ *Hideki Matsuyama Wins the Masters With a Groundbreaking Performance. Matsuyama led the final round from start to finish at Augusta National, becoming the first Asian-born man to win the Masters. Nytimes.com.*

"Asian Hate Crime" **90** RN.
"Asian American" **90** RN.

   Deshaun Watson was later suspended for 11 games and fined $5 million. Football is 11 on 11, and 11 is the 5th prime number. This all coming on the back of him being traded to the Browns. The news came August 18th, 2022, which was exactly **338** days after his September 14, 2021 birthday, and he will be eligible to return on December 4, 2022. December 4th will be the **338th** day of the year. And on December 4th, 2022 the Browns are scheduled to play against Deshaun Watson's old team, the Houston Texans. August 18th is *27* days before his birthday, and December 4th is the day that leaves *27* days in the year.

Black = 11 N.

Ritual = 27 N.
Race = *27* AO.

   UFC fans will remember when Khabib picked up his **29th** win against "Gaethje". Gaethje was 22-2 going into the fight, before the fight took place Khabib mockingly stated he would "choke him out". Khabib did end up choking him out in the 2nd round by way of "Triangle Choke", which set Justin Gaethje to <u>22-3</u>. Coincidentally enough Khabib's father died <u>3</u> months and <u>22</u> days before the fight took place on July 3rd, 2020. Which is a date that could be written *7-3*, relating to the Gematria for "sacrifice". Instead of counting it as 3 months and 22 days later you could state it as *114* days, interesting in light of his fathers death being contributed to "Covid-19 Complications"

"Gaethje" **29** N. (**29th** win)
"Triangle Choke" <u>223</u> RAO.

"Sacrifice" *73* AO.
Khabib's father died on 7-3

"Covid-19 Complications" *114* RN.
Khabib's father died of "Covid-19 Complications" *114* days before the fight.

"Choke Him Out" 56 N.

In a year rife with *56* riddles this was the obvious clue that Khabib would win, no need to see the future when you realize how the media and players put out their Gematria encoded messages through symbolism and celebrity archetypes. All while the public is none the wiser being unfortunately unaware of Gematria. Think of the days of old when messengers were the only means of long distance communication. The royals and nobles would employ codes or use symbols to communicate their messages to insure even if the messenger would be flayed, their personal information would be protected.

Floyd Mayweather and Connor McGregor got rich from a boxing match that featured the two combat athletes. "Floyd", known as one of if not the g.o.a.t. of boxing. While McGregor, a UFC fighter that was out kick boxed by other UFC fighters, was promising entertainment. Many questioned why Floyd came out of retirement, let alone why he chose "McGregor" as his opponent. Mayweather naturally picked up his 50th win and remained "undefeated" when the fight took place on August 26th.

"Boxer" **26** RN.
"Floyd" **26** N.

"Undefeated" 40 N. 50 RN.

"McGregor" 50 N. 40 RN.

A day before the 9/11 anniversary in 2022, was
UFC 279. There was much promotion and headlines
all week about the "chaos" leading up to the event. ~
The fights took place September 10th, a date that can
be written **10-9**. The main event of Diaz vs Chimaev
fell out while all the fighters reshuffled match ups in
a 'the show must go on' effort. With Nate Diaz,
famous for representing the 209 area code, won his
last fight of his career with 2:09 left in the clock.~
Bizarre Coincidence at UFC 279: Fans Are
Convinced MMA Gods Blessed Nate Diaz After He
Submits Tony Ferguson With 2:09 Minute Remaining
in Round 4. sportsmanor.com.
After the main event, the first question posed by
Joe Rogan "what was it like to come into this fight
after all the **chaos** through this week?". In Gematria
the word "Chaos" sums to **19** N. To date the world is
still recovering from the "chaos" of Covid **19**, which
came **19** years after 2001, when the **19** hijackers
caused chaos on 9/11. To pour salt on the wound the
UFC made a Muslim fighter Khamzat Chimaev the
head of all the controversy over the week after he
had missed weight. After Chimaev won his fight he
stole the mic from Joe, yelling out "I WILL KILL
EVERYONE, ALLAHU AKBAR".

"Chaos" **19** N.

"Nathan Donald Diaz" 67 N. 67 is the **19th** Prime in sequence of Primes.

"Nathan Donald Diaz" *148* AO.
Nate Diaz, born April 16th, his final UFC fight on contract taking place on September 10th, exactly *148* days after his birthday, including the day in the count.

   Wrestling champ Navid Afkari was sentenced to death on *September 7th, 2020* after he participated in protests against the government in Iran. He was charged with "conspiracy" and sadly received 47 lashes, no doubt symbolic. Further curious about the case is that his two other brothers arrested on similar charges had already been released.

"Navid Afkari" **51** N.
"Conspiracy" **51** N.

9/7 Date of death.
"Death" *97* RAO.

   There was a notable tragedy that involved the boxing legend George Foreman and his "daughter" "Freda Foreman". She 'committed suicide' at the age of **42** on March 9th, 2019 which can be written *5-9*. If you count from George Foreman's birthday including the date March 9th in the count, its exactly *59* days after George Foreman's January 10th birthday. She died in "Houston, Texas" and her birthday is on the same day in history as the Million Man March, October 16th the day leaving <u>76</u> days left in the year. The 'George Foreman Grill' even claims it can 'remove up **42**% of fat'.

"Daughter" **42** RN.
"Houston, Texas" **181** AO.
181 is the 42nd Prime Number in sequence of Primes.

"Professional Boxer" *213* AO. 93 RN.
"Black History Month" *213* AO. 93 RN.

"African American" 71 N.
George was 71 at the time of her death

"Slave" <u>*59*</u> AO. <u>76</u> RAO.
"Negro" <u>*59*</u> AO. <u>76</u> RAO.
<u>*59*</u> days after George Foreman's birthday.
Freda's birthday was the day leaving <u>76</u> days left in the year.

    The NHL made headlines when the 1st African American head coach had been signed. These headlines came July <u>5</u>th, 2022, going with the themes of the time and coming <u>5</u> days after the U.S. had appointed their 1st African American woman to the supreme court. Michael James Grier was made the general manager of the "San Jose Sharks" on July 5th. That is exactly a span of *181* days from his January 5th birthday.

"Barack Hussein Obama II" *181* AO.
Obama's birthday is *181* days before the start of Black History Month.
"Black History" *181* RAO.
181 Is the 42nd Prime Number in sequence of Primes.

"San Jose Sharks" 42 N.

MUSIC- Following a pattern of seemingly singing things into existence is the case of the death of major recording artist Prince on April 21st, a date that can be written 4-21. One of his many popular songs was titled, "I Would Die 4 U". U being the 21st letter in the alphabet thus he was dropping the hint or perhaps unknowingly sealing his planned ritual demise.

   Perhaps the biggest album release of 2020 came at the end of October. "Extinction Level Event 2 the Wrath of God" released on October 30th, 2020 which was *164* days after Busta Rhymes May 20th birthday. The first Extinction Level Event album released 22 years ago, which relates to the last song on the album being titled, "Satanic" and don't forget there are 22 chapters in Revelation a book about Extinction events. Keeping the theme of Coronavirus and Event

201 the end title of the album "The Wrath of God" sums to 201. The release of this album coming *49* days before the pope's birthday. The first album released by Busta Rhymes was titled "The Coming" which sums to *49*.

"Extinction Level Event 2 the Wrath of God" *164* N. *164* RN.
Album released **164** days after artists birthday.

"Satanic" <u>22</u> N.
The 2nd album to be titled 'Extinction Level Event', the 1st coming out <u>22</u> years earlier.

"The Coming" *49* N. 149 RAO.
"Revelation" *49* N. 149 RAO.

The extremely coincidental death of "Naya" who is the third actor to fall victim to the "Glee Curse". She was found drowned at "Lake Piru". Her crowning moment as a TV singer came when she preformed her solo rendition of the song with the lyrics,
"If I die young, bury me in satin
Lay me down on a bed of roses
<u>Sink me in the river</u> at dawn
Send me away with the words of a love song
Oh-oh, oh-oh"

"Glee" *79* RAO.

"Murder" *79* AO.
"Naya Marie Rivera" *79* N.

"Naya Rivera" <u>51</u> N.
"Lake Piru" <u>51</u> RN

"Naya" **67** RAO.
"Blood Sacrifice" **67** N.

  "Mac Miller" was a "rapper" born January 19th, a date that can be written <u>1-19</u>, he reportedly died from "*O.D.*" *35* days after the album 'Swimming' released. The album released on the damming date of August 3rd, a date written *8-3* or *3-8*. The cause of the overdose was due to "Fentanyl". His real name was "Malcolm McCormick" which sums to **157** just like his rap alias, and also tying into to the ritual is his last music video for the single 'Self Care' which released on July 12th, 57 days before his September 7th death, a date written *9-7* or *7-9*. At **1:57** in the music video Mac begins to carve a <u>circle</u> into the coffin he is laying in, a circle being required in most teachings to conduct magic. Inside the circle he inscribes "Memento Mori" which translates as "Remember you will die". Both phrases being synced with his death. Just think of the symbolism, obviously in a coffin writing to himself remember you have to die which he does 57 days after the video, which isn't contrary in light of him being

Jewish, reflect back to "Jews", "Moon", and Deuteronomy 5:7. (pg. 89).

"Mac Miller" **157** RAO.
"Malcolm McCormick" **157** AO.
"Memento Mori" **157** RAO.

"Rapper" *38* N.
"Murder" *79* AO. *83* RAO. *38* RN.
"Death" *38* AO. *97* RAO.
"Fentanyl" *97* AO. <u>119</u> RAO. *38* RN.
"Remember You Will Die" *97* N.
9-7 date of his death.
<u>11-9</u> birthday.
3-8 date of his last albums release

"O.D." *35* RAO.
Died *35* days after album release.

   As if the ritual wasn't tight enough after his death there was an album released with songs he had already recorded. "<u>Circles</u> by Mac Miller" came out on January 17th, 2020, interesting they didn't wait two days to release it on his birthday, the joke being that the album released *38* days after the producer Jon Brion's birthday. Notice "Jon Brion" is synced with murder, death, Fentanyl, and Mac Millers <u>1-19</u> birthday.

"Jon Brion" *97* AO. <u>119</u> RAO.

  A popular metal band that brandishes occult concepts is Slipknot. They released the album 'All Hope Is Gone' on August 20, 2008. August 20th, 2008 has a date numerology of 38 (8 + 20 + 2 + 0 + 0 + 8= <u>38</u>). After the albums release on May 24th, 2010 Paul Grey died at age <u>38</u>, only *46* days after his April 8th birthday. The second song on the album is titled "Gematria (The Killing Name)". The song is **6:02** long relating to the Gematria of the word "sacrifice". The second member of the band to die was Joey Jordison, passing away on July 26th, 2021 a date with <u>38</u> numerology (7 + 26 + 2 + 0 + 2 + 1= <u>38</u>). Joey Jordison was *46* years old at the time of his death. If one rearranges the letters in the name Slipknot, it can render *Klipots. (klipa,* singular*)*, which translates from Hebrew as "husks" or "shells,". Metaphysical barriers between ourselves and the Light of the Creator that we, ourselves, have created through our own selfish actions. It is what keeps us from receiving all meant for us, or stalling away the feeling of fulfillment.

"Gematria" <u>38</u> N.
"Killing" <u>38</u> N.
"Murder" <u>83</u> RAO. <u>38</u> RN.
"Death" <u>38</u> AO.
"Klipot" <u>83</u> AO.

"Faustian Bargain" **62** N.
"Sacrifice" *46* N. **62** RN.
(Genesis chapter *46* begins with a sacrifice)

Torey Lanez was arrested on October 8th, 2020 for the shooting of Meg the Stallion on July 12th, 2020. From the date of the shooting to October 8th is **88** days. Of course Torey Lanez real name "Daystar Peterson" sums to 88. Not unlike the word "rapper" which is what Torey Lanez is famous for being. The arrest came *74* days after his July 27th birthday.

"Daystar" **88** AO.
"Daystar Peterson" **88** RN.
"Rapper" *74* AO. **88** RAO.

Another rapper in the headlines around that time was "Saint Dog" who died at the inconspicuous age of <u>44</u>. Not arbitrary was the death of Atlanta underground D.J. Black N Mild at age <u>44</u> from Coronavirus. There were reports of the popular rapper Young Dolph being shot and killed on November 17th, 2021, the day leaving <u>44</u> days left in the year. Earlier in the year on February 1st, 2021, it was reported that **D**ustin **D**iamond from 'Saved by the Bell' had died at age <u>44</u>. <u>D</u>ustin <u>D</u>iamond died 2-1-2021, the numerology for that date was 2+1+20+21= <u>44</u>. On that same date 2-1-2021 CNN put out an article claiming "U.S. death toll from coronavirus hits 440,000". On April 20ᵗʰ, 2021 there were reports of "44 killed in stampede during Lag B'Omer celebrations in Israel." On March 31ˢᵗ, 2022 multiple news outlets reported on a shooting that took place in an office building, where a 44 year old killed 4 people at the City of Orange Business Complex. The killers of Ahmaud Arbery were sentenced 44 days after pleading guilty to murder. Ahmaud Arbery was a black man jogging down the street before being senselessly shot by two white men driving in the area. The mayor of Hyattsville, Maryland, Kevin Ward reportedly committed suicide at age 44, January 25ᵗʰ, 2022. Famous body building competitor Cedric McMilan dropped dead at age 44, April 12, 2022. The number 4 is associated with death being that in Japanese the word for 'death' and the word for '4' are pronounced the same way. 4 is spelled 四 and Death is spelled 死, the English transliteration for both is 'Shi'.

"Kill" 44 AO. *17* N.
D is the 4ᵗʰ Letter in the alphabet. A headstone on a grave is an elongated 'D'.
Death, Die, Destroy, De; remove, the opposite of. Meanwhile the prefix De is spoken as simply D. We see Death as a Doorway to a new Dimension, and practically all doorways are 4 sided.
"Lag B'Omer" 44 RN.

On November 10th, 2020 "DJ Spinbad" passed away, November 10th is comedian Sinbad's birthday. DJ Spinbad was **46** years old at the time of his death and Sinbad was 64.

"DJ Spinbad" <u>79</u> AO. <u>34</u> N.
"Murder" <u>79</u> AO. <u>34</u> N.
"Sacrifice" **46** N.

   Da Baby's brother reportedly committed suicide on November 3rd, 2020 which was **49** days before Da Baby's December 22nd birthday. This news came out just weeks after the release of his new album titled "Blame <u>it</u> on Baby". I wonder what the 'it' he is referring to is. If you measure from his previous birthday December 22nd, 2019 up to November 3rd, 2020 it is <u>317</u> days. Now <u>317</u> is the <u>66</u>th Prime Number in sequence of Primes, and in light of his brother dying what is the most famous story of brothers in the bible, "Cain and Abel"? *"One month after I signed & dropped my debut album Baby On Baby in 2019, my lil brother hit me & told me my daddy was found dead in his crib.". DaBaby Shares His Devastation After His Father's Death. Urbandislandz.com.*

"Blame it on Baby" **49** N.
"Cain and Abel" <u>66</u> AO.

From "Kobe Bean Bryant" scoring 81 points in a game to Nya Riveria gaining popularity for singing "drown me in the river", it is clear that; 1. there is a theme of using numbers relevant to their names and birthdays 2. Implementing the use of these numbers to coincide with something they did for popularity, fame, fortune. 3. Like a double edged the sword 'their numbers up' and they exit the stage the same way they entered, by the numbers. If the star dies the company behind their rise to stardom still benefits as their imagery and riddles perpetuate in the minds eye of the masses. Unless the common man's awareness is brought to consciously reject the ritualistic news, sports, and celebrity cycle, society will continue to worship the riddlers.

KJV Revelation 18:4 And I heard another voice from heaven, saying, Come out of her, my people, that ye be not partakers of her sins, and that ye receive not of her plagues.

369

"If you only knew the magnificence of the 3, 6 and 9, then you would have <u>a key to the universe</u>."
– Nikola Tesla

"A Key To The Universe" <u>79</u> N. <u>236</u> RAO.
"Three, Six, And Nine" <u>79</u> N. <u>236</u> RAO.

We understand that we didn't create math, we discovered it. Mathematics is a Universal law. Mathematics was and still is one of the most powerful and important languages, used and expounded for centuries by great minds. Mathematics or numbers play a part in all creations. Every human being, everyone, needs mathematics in their day-to-day life. Notice Nikola states this is **a key** to the universe, meaning singular in that there are more than one. Just as I stated in the introduction Gematria is a key, Mathematics is a law.

The reason Tesla called these divine numbers is due to the properties they represent in our mathematic systems. In particular, note that a circle has 360° and $(3 + 6 + 0 = 9)$. His short quote can inspire positive inquiries into the centrality of these numbers in our universe.

"What Numbers Prove God's Existence" **369** AO.
"God What Are Your Favorite Numbers?" **369** AO.

There must have been at least some reason that Tesla was obsessed with equations and numbers? In Vortex Math you follow a specific pattern and see, starting with 1, and doubling it (1+1) we got 2, again, doubling 2 (2+2) we got 4. Further doubling 32 (32+32) we got 64 and summing up 6+4 gave us 10 which again summing up the two digits gave us 1. If you keep following this pattern, It will always give us the digits 1, 2, 4, 5, 7, 8.

Notice how 3, 6, and 9 are not in this pattern. Scientist Marko Rodin (Discoverer of Vortex Maths) believes these numbers represent a vector from the third to fourth dimension which he calls a "flux field." This field is supposed to be higher dimensional energy that influences the energy circuit of the other six points (1, 2, 4, 5, 7, 8). If you take these 3 numbers (3, 6 and 9), starting with 3 and doubling it ($3 + 3 = 6$; $6 + 6 = 12$; $9 + 9 = 18 = 1+8=9$.), you will find that 9 always rules itself, thus 9 governs both sides of the equation.

Let's say there are 2 opposites, call them light and dark if you want to. They are like the North and the South poles of a magnet.

One side is 1, 2, and 4; the other side is 8, 7 and 5; Just like electricity, everything in The Universe is a stream between these 2 polar sides, like a swinging pendulum: 1, 2, 4, 8, 7, 5, 1, 2... Close your eyes to imagine the movement.

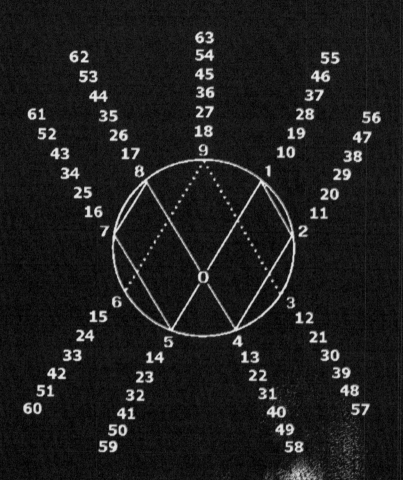

Math Meditations- There are two different forms for this method. Method 1. will be the shorter method for the busy individual. Method 2. is for the individual willing to set aside some time. You could do a 3rd method combining the two. The convenient thing about this practice is that it only takes the dedication of one day to complete.

Method 1.

- First, from the time you awake up until noon, say a positive affirmation or bible verse that inspires you, at 3 separate times.
  EX: "I will appreciate life today."
  Deuteronomy 6:5 "Love the Lord your God with all your heart."

- Second, from noon till 6, say a negative affirmation that you want to change about yourself or a bible verse rebuking you, 6 separate times.
  EX: "I need to stop being hateful"
  Leviticus 19:18 "You will not take vengeance or hold a grudge"

- Lastly, from 6 to the time you fall asleep, say a statement for the benefit of someone else, or a bible verse about being compassionate, 9 separate times.
  EX. "May everyone find peace"

Psalm 115:14 "May The Lord give <u>you</u> increase, You and your children."
Replace '<u>you</u>' with the name of someone you wish to bless.

Method 2.

- First, from the time you awake up until noon, write down 3 times, a positive affirmation or bible verse that inspires you.
  EX: "I will appreciate life today."
  Deuteronomy 6:5 "Love the Lord your God with all your heart."

- Second, from noon till 6, write down 6 times, a negative affirmation that you want to change about yourself or a bible verse rebuking you.
  EX: "I need to stop being hateful" Leviticus 19:18 "You will not take vengeance or hold a grudge"

- Lastly, from 6 to the time you fall asleep, write down 9 times, a benefit of someone else, or a bible verse about being compassionate.
  EX. "May everyone find peace"
  Psalm 115:14 "May The Lord give <u>you</u> increase, You and your children."
  Replace '<u>you</u>' with the name of someone you wish to bless.

'Detailing 9'

It has been demonstrated to this point how 9 is a kind of leader or governor in terms of vortex math. Active people with strong 9 associations in their name and birthdates are often seen as those that "lead in deed", their intuitive communication skills make it seem that they don'y give orders but rather suggest the best course of action. The number 9 can be associated with completion, however because it is last of the single digits it symbolizes a kind of completion, and not necessarily a finished perfection like 10. This is why Pythagoras saw the number 9 as an omen of bad luck, just short of perfection. The relative symbol of completion can be observed in the human gestation period, where an average pregnancy lasts approximately 9 months. 9 as a symbol and ignoring its number properties does resemble a sphere or heavenly influence touching or projecting down to the world below. From the spiritual world a soul manifests coming to the physical world by way of the 9 month pregnancy. Pythagoras was particularly fascinated by this number, comparing it to God, just as he did with the number 4.

"**Nine**" 24 **N**. 21 **RN**.
"Four" 24 **N** 21 **RN**

"Pythagoras" **49 N**.

The <u>N</u> cipher is often referred to as the **Pythagorean** cipher, **RN** would be Reverse Pythagorean.
To date, the latest Perfect Number discovered came in 2016, and it being the **49th** in sequence of Perfect Numbers. In the Old Testament there are a total of 48 male prophets, Jesus in his divine nature is seen as the last one to be God's messenger thus being the **49th** male prophet.

"<u>**Numerology**</u>" <u>55</u> N. <u>44</u> RN.

"<u>Fifty Five</u>" 108 AO. 54 N. 135 RAO. 45 RN
(1+0+8=**9** AO.) (5+4=**9** N.) (1+3+5=**9** RAO.)
(4+5=**9** RN.)

"<u>Forty Four</u>" 144 AO. 54 N. 99 RAO. 45 RN.
(1+4+4=**9** AO.) (5+4=**9** N.) (9+9=18.)(1+8=**9** RAO.)
(4+5=**9** RN.)

<u>55+44=**99**</u>

In numerology, there are some traits unique to 9. First, if you add 9 to any number, it will preserve the numerology it had before you added 9. EX: If you add 9 to 1, it becomes 10, breaking down to 1. Then if you add 9 to 2, it sums to 11, breaking down to 2. Even more, if you add 9 to 3, it sums to 12, breaking down to 3, and so on. There is no exception to this rule. That is why in the N. and RN. ciphers, each letter that is spaced out by 9 spaces, breaks down to the same digit. For example, A, the 1st letter, J the 10th letter, and S the 19th letter, each equating back to number 1. With the N. cipher its the same with B the 2nd letter, K the 11th letter, and T the 20th letter. You might have also noticed that in N. and in RN. 'I' and 'R' are the only digits breaking down to 9. The second thing that makes number 9 special is that if you multiply any number by 9, it will take on numerology of 9. Notice the following examples.

$9 \times 1 = 9$

$9 \times 2 = 18$ (18 is 1+8=9)

$9 \times 3 = 27$ (27 is 2+7=9)

$9 \times 369 = 3,321$ (3,321 is 3+3+2+1=9)

In Kabbalah, the 9th sphere, Yesod (purple) is the foundation of the universe. We are able to trace cause and effect of scientific laws so detailed these days, yet, tracing the root cause, or initial cause that established laws themselves seems impossible to discern. Only once the formless forces above have transferred into this space of nothingness can they then be 're-materialized' in the kingdom below. Nine is one step before ten, one place before completion. If ten is the number of perfection then nine symbolizes completion but it does not include the sum of all (הכל). The Tree of Life as a symbol is an extensive field for mathematical operations, theological symbols, abstract thinking, and geometric divisions. Symbols of seemingly abstract value shouldn't be overlooked as they hold the potential to embody the spiritual forces that operate behind them. A symbols very existence is proof that, even if we do not understand principles today, they have been there, and they will remain in the future.

55 is the 10th Triangular Number in sequence of Triangular Numbers.

1+2+3+4+5+6+7+8+9+10= 55

הכל   55 HG (All)

"The Significance Of The Three Six And Nine"
183 N.

"The Infinite String Of Fibonacci Numbers"
183 N.

"Numbers, Their Occult Power And Mystic Virtues"
183 N.

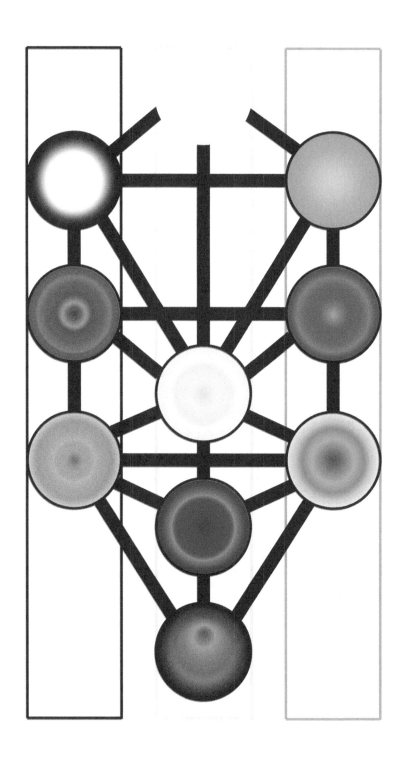

54, 45, 4+5 or 4.5?

"Numbers are the highest degree of knowledge. It is knowledge itself."
– Plato

"Geometry"
108 AO. <u>45</u> N. 108 RAO. 36 RN.
1+0+8=**9** AO. 4+5=**9** N. 1+0+8=**9** RAO. 3+6=**9** RN.

These two numbers just cant seem to stay away from each other. As the title eludes any way you wanna break it down or add it up it comes to 9. Is it coincidence that the two most popular ammo sizes for handguns are 9mm and .45 acp? These numbers show up around many key words seen through the book thus far.

5+4=9.   4+5=9.   4.5+5.4= 9.9.
(1+2+3+4+5+6+7+8+9= 45). <u>45</u> is the 9th Triangular Number in sequence of Triangular Numbers.
"Geometry" <u>45</u> N.
"Holy Bible" <u>45</u> N. <u>45</u> RN.
"The Bible" <u>45</u> RN
אדם   <u>45</u> HG (Adam)
"All is Number" <u>45</u> N.
"Α Β Γ Δ Ε Ζ Η Θ F I K Λ M N Ξ O Π P Σ T Y Φ X Ψ Ω"   <u>4005</u> GI
"Numerology" 55 N. 44 RN.
55+44=99

"Fifty Five" **54** N. <u>45</u> RN.
"Forty Four" **54** N. <u>45</u> RN.

"HaShem**"** *54 AO.*
"Good and Evil" **54** N. **54** RN.

Definitions

Gematria- is an alphanumeric code of assigning a numerical value to a name, word or phrase based on its letters. A single word can yield multiple values depending on the cipher used.

Propaganda- **1** especially of a biased or misleading nature, used to promote or publicize a particular political cause or point of view. **2** a committee of cardinals of the Roman Catholic Church responsible for foreign missions, founded in 1622 by Pope Gregory XV.

Synchronicity- The simultaneous occurrence of events which appear significantly related but have no discernible causal connection.

Ritual- **1** rituals (plural noun) a religious or solemn ceremony consisting of a series of actions performed according to a prescribed order. **2** performance the prescribed order of performing a ceremony **3** protocol a series of actions or type of behavior regularly and invariably followed by someone.

Energy- **1** the strength and vitality required for sustained physical or mental activity. **2** power derived from the utilization of physical or chemical resources, especially to provide light and heat or to work machines.

Pattern- **1** a repeated decorative design **2** figure a model or design used as a guide in needlework and other crafts. **3** an example for others to follow.

Program- **1** provide (a computer or other machine) with coded instructions for the automatic performance of a task. **2** set · fix · arrange cause (a person or animal) to behave in a predetermined way **3** broadcast (an item)"

MATHEMATICAL

Triangular Number- The Nth triangular number is equal to the sum of the N numbers from 1 to N.

Prime Number- A number that is indivisible except by 1 and N.

Fibonacci Number- a series of numbers in which each number (Fibonacci number) is the sum of the two preceding numbers. The simplest is the series 1, 1, 2, 3, 5, 8, etc.

Perfect Numbers- A perfect number, a positive integer that is equal to the sum of its proper divisors. The smallest perfect number is 6, which is the sum of 1, 2, and 3. Other perfect numbers are 28, 496, and 8,128.

HERMETIC

Mentalism- *The All is mind; The Universe is Mental.*

Correspondence- *As above, so below; as below, so above. As within, so without; as without, so within.*

Vibration- *Nothing rests; Everything moves; Everything vibrates.*

Polarity- *Everything is dual; Everything has poles; Everything has its pair of opposites; Like and unlike are the same; Opposites are identical in nature, but different in degree; Extremes meet; All truths, are but half-truths; All paradoxes may be reconciled.*

Rhythm- *Everything flows, out and in; Everything has its tides; All things rise and fall; The pendulum swing manifests in everything; The measure of the swing to the right is the measure of the swing to the left; Rhythm compensates.*

Cause and Effect- *Every cause has its effect; Every effect has its cause; Everything happens according to law' Chance is but a name for law not recognized' There are many planes of causation, but nothing escapes the law.*

Gender- *Gender is in everything; Everything has its masculine and feminine principles; Gender manifests on all planes.*

Further Reading

1. The Book of Formation- Akiba Ben Joseph

2. Letters and Numbers- Zachary K. Hubbard

3. The Esoteric Structure of the Alphabet- Alvin Boyd Kuhn

4. The Secret Teachings of All Ages- Manly P. Hall

5. The Sacred Magic of the Qabbalah- Manly P. Hall

6. The Mystical Qabalah- Dion Fortune

7. Illuminations: Mystical Meditations on the Hebrew Alphabet- Dolores Ashcroft-Nowicki

8. Kabbalah the Harmony of Opposites- W. J. Colville

9. The Kybalion- Three Initiates

10. The Geometric Genesis- Frank C. Higgins

11. The Tree of Evil- William G. Gray

12. Jewish Wisdom in the Numbers- Osher Chaim Levene with Rabbi Yehoshua Hartman

13. Kabbalah the Way of the Jewish Mystic- Perle Besserman

14. Astral Worship- J.H. Hill

15. The Kabala Of Numbers (1920)

Hebrew	Name	Transliteration
א	Alef	Silent
בּ	Beyt	B
ג	Gimel	G
ד	Daled	D
ה	Hey	H
ו	Vav	V
ז	Zayin	Z
ח	Chet	HH or CHK
ט	Tet	T
י	Yod	Y
כּ	Kaph	K or KH
ל	Lamed	L
ם מ	Mem	M
נ	Nun	N
ס	Sameh	S
ע	Ayin	Silent
פ ף פּ	Pey	P or PH (F)
צ	Tsade	TS or TZ
ק	Quph	Q
ר	Resh	R
שׁ שׂ	Sin/ Shin	S or SH
ת	Tav	T

Greek	Name	Transliteration
A	Alpha	A
B	Beta	B
Γ	Gamma	G
Δ	Delta	D
E	Epsilon	E
Z	Zeta	Z
H	Eta	H
Θ	Theta	Q
I	Iota	I
K	Kappa	K
Λ	Lambda	L
M	Mu	M
N	Nu	N
Ξ	Xi	X
O	Omicron	O
Π	Pi	P
P	Rho	R
Σ	Sigma	S
T	Tau	T
Y	Upsilon	U
Φ	Phi	F
X	Chi	C
Ψ	Psi	Y
Ω	Omega	W

GEMATRIA GEMS
Secret Code In The Bible Across Languages

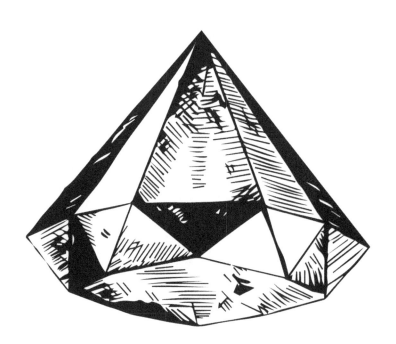

Made in the USA
Las Vegas, NV
05 October 2024

96347015R00138